This is a book grounded in both knowledge and experience. It will be a valuable resource for all who want to explore the riches of the Christian faith.
Fr. Kevin Smith, Priest Administrator, Shrine of our Lady of Walsingham

This is an important book and would be useful reading for every teacher or Headteacher in our church schools and indeed for all Governors. For clergy it will be a useful book to recommend and to use as a resource when teaching the basics of the faith. Just as schools are discovering and returning to a knowledge-based curriculum so as churches we need to recognise the basics that every Christian should understand and know. John-Francis brings the wisdom and sensitivity of a life time of spiritual direction and ministry to others to the task and presents the faith wisely and with great charm.
The Rev. Richard Peers, Director of Education, Diocese of Liverpool

The author weaves teachings drawn from scripture and the saints with reflections on his own life and ministry, creating an approachable and profound guide to the Christian faith. This is a book for the person seeking a faith rooted in tradition and open to the challenges of real life.
Br Christopher John SSF, Minister General

Fr John-Francis has the gift of the story teller. His reminiscences make complex ideas simple. This is the perfect introduction to Christianity for the general reader.
Fr Mund Cargill Thompson SCP, Vice Rector (Evangelism), Society of Catholic Priests.

John-Francis draws on the "wisdom of the ages" to introduce faith in an accessible and engaging way. And he also
draws on his own long experience as Franciscan, priest, and
spiritual director to ground this tradition in the reality of one
life. Questions and suggestions for reflection help the reader
to apply what they read to their own journey of faith, whatever their starting point.

Sr Helen Julian CSF, Minister General

John-Francis draws on a life-times reflection as a pilgrim on
a faith journey. His own journey has taken him from living
in community, encouraging vocations, to pastoring a community as a parish priest. Now, as an experienced spiritual
director and retreat conductor, his teaching and pastoral
ministry combine in this accessible introduction to the
Christian Faith. In the same vein as Michael Ramsey's lovely
book 'Introducing the Christian Faith,' this book is both
simple yet profound and allows the reader to be immersed in
the great traditions of the Church, whilst making connections
with the world around us. As Jesus himself says, "Every scribe
who has been trained for the kingdom of heaven is like the
master of a household who brings out of his treasure what is
new and what is old."

*Fr Carl Turner, Rector, St. Thomas Church, Fifth Avenue,
New York, USA*

The Mystery of Faith

Exploring Christian Belief

John-Francis Friendship

Christmas 2019

CANTERBURY
PRESS
Norwich

© John-Francis Friendship 2019

First published in 2019 by the Canterbury Press Norwich
Editorial office
3rd Floor, Invicta House
108–114 Golden Lane
London EC1Y 0TG, UK
www.canterburypress.co.uk

Canterbury Press is an imprint of Hymns Ancient & Modern Ltd
(a registered charity)

Hymns Ancient & Modern® is a registered trademark of
Hymns Ancient & Modern Ltd
13A Hellesdon Park Road, Norwich,
Norfolk NR6 5DR, UK

Scripture quotations are from the New Revised Standard Version
of the Bible, Anglicized Edition, copyright © 1989, 1995 by
the Division of Christian Education of the National Council
of the Churches of Christ in the USA. Used by permission.
All rights reserved.

British Library Cataloguing in Publication data

A catalogue record for this book is available
from the British Library

978 1 78622 180 3

Typeset by Regent Typesetting
Printed and bound in Great Britain by
CPI Group (UK) Ltd

This book is dedicated to
Mary of Walsingham,
Mother of Jesus
who, having been encountered by an angel,
pondered in her heart,
and gave birth to the Word.

Contents

REDEEMER

Acknowledgements

I'm very grateful to Canterbury Press for inviting me to write this book and for the confidence and assistance offered by Christine Smith and her colleagues. It's the fruit of many years exploring Faith and the consequence of the help people have shown me on that journey. It's also a reflection of my interest in evangelism stemming from my years in Franciscan Religious Life, when I was involved in many parish, school and diocesan missions, and I hope it will be of some use to those exploring the vast richness of the Christian Faith.

Thanks to Anna Cole, Sue Dunbar-Silk, Fr Edmund Cargill-Thompson, John and Sue Heath, Chris Marlowe, Br Christopher John SSF and the Revd Jackie Turner for their helpful comments. To members of the congregation of All Saints, Blackheath for their observations, and to the Revd Dr John Cullen, Bishop Martyn Jarrett, Nicola Mason, Fr Simon Robinson SMMS and Sr Helen Julian CSF for their detailed critique.

After having had to put up with me writing one book I'm enormously grateful to my partner, Chris Marlowe, for his generous support as I attempted to explore and express some of the riches of the Christian Faith which, I trust, might be of use to the Church.

Foreword

I have never felt more urgent about the importance of the Christian Gospel for the world. I am getting older. I have seen in others the pressure of the time of their lives running out. John-Francis must have been feeling something of this as he set down this account of the fundamentals of the Christian faith. But I mean more than that. I was born in the 1950s into the post-war optimism of a world in which things could only get better. The twentieth century ended hopefully with a growing internationalism, the fall of the Berlin wall, an acceptance of our God-given diversity and the end of apartheid in South Africa. In 2001 this changed on 9/11 and our present century is proving very much more complex to navigate. Religious faith, which the secularists of the twentieth century thought would die out, has gained a new lease of life-giving identity, meaning, purpose and potency for better as well as for worse.

The political pressure in the UK following the Referendum in 2016 to leave the EU is very disturbing. It won't end when we have successfully changed the relationship with our immediate neighbours in the European Union. We will need to rediscover what it means to be English/Scottish/Welsh/Northern Irish, many of us from other parts of the world as well, British, European even if not part of the European Union, and global citizens on this fragile earth.

All over the world a new nationalism has been emerging in which people are wanting to assert their identities in smaller, more distinctive cultural, ethnic and political units. Patriotism is good because in order to belong everywhere we need to belong somewhere, and it is good to love our country. But the love of the particular is to teach us the love of everywhere and everyone in this wonderfully diverse earth. Charity begins at home but does not stop there.

In our world, we are encouraged to choose whatever best suits us from the range of alternative facts. Truth no longer counts for much because it can be difficult to establish. It seems acceptable for political leaders to put themselves and their country first as if the rest of us don't matter. In response to the greatest migration of people since World War Two, countries are turning in on themselves and building walls to keep people out. We are telling stories to each other that are fearful and anxious. We think the gifts of creation are ours to keep rather than to use and steward for the good of all.

Of course, we need to take care to distinguish our context from the text of the Christian faith, but it does feel deeply urgent for us to learn again what it is to love God and love our neighbour as ourselves and care for the earth, our common home. According to St Paul, faith, hope and love last for ever. Truth, peace and justice are the values of the kingdom of God which Jesus said is very near. These are what really matter, and they are accessed through the riches of Christianity.

St Augustine, writing in similarly turbulent times at the end of the fourth century, said that people travel to see the world and pass over the mystery of themselves without a thought. He could have been writing for us. John-Francis sets out here the fundamentals of Christianity in such a way as to establish and deepen the faith of those seeking greater understanding. I warmly welcome this book because it will help you to know the riches of Christianity and to better follow in the way of Jesus Christ. It is a deeply urgent task, never more important.

+ *Nicholas Holtam*
Bishop of Salisbury

Introduction

'What's it all about?'

I wonder if you've ever been sitting quietly, minding your own business without a care in the world – maybe gazing absent-mindedly out of a train window – when you've suddenly had that fleeting thought creep up on you – what's it all about? Life, I mean. What's it all about? Is it about making money? Experiencing all the pleasures the world can give? Raising kids ... being kind to people? Does life belong only to the strong, confident and fearless? Is getting my own way what it's all about? Or is there something more? Does life have a purpose and can that really be summed up as 'eat, drink and be merry (for tomorrow we die)'?

These were questions I found myself asking when I was 16. Having begun work I needed to make some new friends and broaden my horizons, so my mother suggested I try the youth club she'd heard about at the local Church of England parish church. I did, and after a while was invited to attend Midnight Mass, an invitation I accepted and an experience that proved to be the first great turning point in my life. For as the Mass proceeded, I found myself in floods of tears – 16 years old and crying – for what?

As I look back, I can sense a door had opened onto a world I didn't know existed. But it was one I longed, somewhere deep inside, to connect with; a world beyond my understanding where God holds all in his loving regard and where I would find my true home.

Slowly I realized I wanted to receive Holy Communion, to feed on him who I sensed was present in the Sacrament. That's when the journey consciously began because I found I needed to be baptized and confirmed, which involved attending classes on Faith – and these opened so many other questions.

If I knew then what was in store for me would I have continued? Absolutely! Being a Christian is to be on a journey, a pilgrimage, which like Abram in the Old Testament (Gen. 12) involves saying 'yes' to something or someone who invites us to step out from the confines of our known world into a new world where we are gazed on with the eyes of Love. It's a way walked by saints, known and unknown, who journey with us and whose prayers aid us. We begin where we begin and gradually set our sights on what has been called the heavenly City, the 'New Jerusalem', which is above and beyond us.

I had no sudden conversion experience but was gradually drawn more deeply into the mystery we call God. Of course, it wasn't straightforward – few journeys are. My own has woven in and out, sometimes forwards, sometimes backwards. At times nothing much seems to be happening or one just stops in order to rest. Ancients invented a symbol for this known as the labyrinth: an irregular path spiralling around – sometimes you seem close to the centre, at others apparently far away – until, finally, you come to the destination: that heavenly Jerusalem. There's a passage in the New Testament Letter to the Hebrews which sums it all up:

(We look to) Jesus the pioneer and perfecter of our faith, who for the sake of the joy that was set before him endured the cross, disregarding the shame, and has taken his seat at the right hand of the throne of God. (Hebrews 12.2)

Picture language telling us it's Jesus we seek and Jesus we follow and Jesus who is our inspiration and guide on the way.

Who's the book for?

This book is meant for anyone interested to know more about the Christian faith. It's not meant to be a philosophical tome, intellectual essay or theological reflection on society, but an exploration – a meditation – on some of the fundamentals of that Faith, how it connects with life and what it has to offer. I've included a number of reflective questions from time to time so the book could be used as a resource for a Confirmation course or study group – you'll find more about this in Appendix 3.

Many have little time for religion although some are happy to consider themselves 'spiritual'. Yet Christianity has developed an amazing civilization – not perfect but rich in human and spiritual insights which, for 2,000 years, has inspired musicians and artists, sculptors and poets to express the heights and depths opened up by faith – the mysteries of life revealed by one Man (Jesus) who died so tragically on a hill in Palestine.

Sadly, the symbol for the Passion, Death and Resurrection of Christ has become – for many – a chocolate bunny you buy from your local store at Easter. But questions about the nature of life don't go away – 'Is there any purpose to it all?' 'Why do good people suffer?' 'I'm doing so much but life seems empty.' 'What will happen when I die?' 'Why do I feel worthless?' All these and more are matters with which the Church has long struggled. But the wisdom of the ages can be inaccessible to those cut off from these ancient roots as they lose interest in religion.

For 2,000 years, we engaged with the Christian story; to the call to live for the glory of God, to realize ourselves as part of God's good creation. To love neighbour as self; not to make money our god and to show compassion to those in need. To serve the other, seeking to make a difference and not just a quick buck, and to beware the gilded cage of 'success' and the lure of wealth. To discover the glory for which we're created, a glory realized in relationship with God. But what, now, is the 'overarching narrative' – the 'metanarrative' – for our society?

At heart this is a book about how we can enter more deeply into that relationship with the One in whose 'image' we are created. I was fortunate to have been adopted as a baby and grew up with loving parents, although there were times when I wasn't sure about that. Once, when I was a young Franciscan, my Novice Guardian observed: 'You didn't just "happen", you were chosen', and then sent me home for a weekend for no other reason than to see (with the eye of the heart) how I was loved. Not in the way I might have wanted but in the way they could, which proved a real eye-opener and sometimes I've suggested to others they might do something similar.

So, this is a book about the heart of who we are and how that can be nurtured and nourished. Many have no sense that in the centre of their being they have a soul which bears the image of God; but to have lost that awareness is to have lost something of profound significance in understanding what it means to be human. For we bear such beauty within us, a beauty indelibly stamped upon us, a reflection of Divine beauty; a beauty longing to be realized and cherished. There's even a term for this – *theosis* – being so at one with God that we're aglow with Divine life. It all depends on what you believe.

Christianity and life in all its fullness

That's what this book ultimately concerns and how faith, and developing our religious imagination, enables that. Plenty of people say they have no faith, but you can't live without it. Faith that love will conquer, compassion will make us more human and death doesn't have the final word. Faith isn't something you suddenly 'get' or catch as you might a cold, it's something you begin to live with and by, something that expands the heart and makes life richer, more complete. Faith and trust and hope are good bedfellows. As Joan Chittister OSB wrote:

> *It is at the point where we desire to see,*
> *because deep down our hearts believe*
> *what our minds cannot explain, that faith sets in.*[1]

What's this book about?

I want to explore how Christian belief, which has nurtured and nourished people for 2,000 years, is still relevant even though many think it the preserve of fools, bigots or mad fundamentalists. But this being human involves inhabiting a metaphorical 'house', some of whose passageways lead to the place where God abides. Many ignore those ways or simply refuse to enter them. It's a 'house' with cellars and attics containing a hoard of wisdom for us to explore; some contain treasures and others offer places of profound refreshment, yet the doorways to those have often become forgotten, covered in cobwebs – 'we don't want to go there, what's the point?'

Yet to lose touch with our roots – with our soul – cuts us off from so much of that ancient wisdom and can result in us becoming shallow people satisfied by superficialities. Loss of the Christian narrative denies us its wellspring and can even be destabilizing, so we'll be gazing into the depths of the 'well' of faith where we'll find that it's God who is looking for us from those depths:

> *Understanding is the reward of faith.*
> *Therefore do not seek to understand in order to believe,*
> *but believe that you may understand.*[2]

What you'll find in these pages

Here are reflections on very basic Christian beliefs, how they've been lived out and how others have responded to them. To give that some shape I've used the form of what's known as the 'Apostles' Creed', which you'll find at the end of this Introduction. But this isn't an exploration of the Creed, rather an exploration of Faith using its themes.

'Creed' simply means to believe and trust and this one was developed by the early Church for those preparing for baptism. It wasn't written by the apostles but was intended to convey the essence of the Faith they proclaimed and which they had the duty to pass on. It isn't a set of rules to be obeyed and doesn't go into any explanation – it simply says: *This is what we believe*, binding together in time and space all who accept it. Christians need no more to define their faith.

When, in the Orthodox Liturgy of St John Chrysostom, the Creed is about to be affirmed the priest says:

> *Let us love one another, so that with one mind we may confess.*

To which the people respond:

> *The Father, and the Son and the Holy Spirit, the Trinity, one in substance and undivided.*

Reminding us that it's an affirmation of what enables right living.

Belief opens other dimensions of life. At its best, religion doesn't attempt to provide simple answers to life's complex questions (though some think it does), but to illuminate the pathway whereby we can discover the truth of who we are: how we realize ourselves, with our unique wonder, as part of a vast whole which finds itself embraced in the mystery of God.

True religion is not about possessing the truth. No religion does that. It is rather an invitation into a journey that leads one toward the mystery of God. Idolatry is religion pretending that it has all the answers.[3]

Much of my life these days involves sitting and listening to people who are trying to make sense of all the movements that happen within them as they seek to give attention to God. It's called 'spiritual direction' and you'll find some notes on this ministry in Appendix 1. There are also lots of biblical references, indicated like this: 1 Corinthians 3.1(ff.), which indicates the First Letter to the Corinthians, chapter 3, verse(s) 1 (and following verses).

Christianity isn't simply about trying to be a 'good' person, keeping a set of rules or being saved from adversity. It's about realizing there's a journey to be made to become what God is calling us to be. About living by the faith that Jesus lived by and which has provided a guide to all who've sought to follow him. It's a way of life, not just something we do on Sunday.

As we begin let's look at the one question we can't avoid – just what do we understand by that three-letter word: God? Because everything that follows depends on that. You don't have to begin there – you might want to skip to another chapter, but I'm going to plunge in at the deep end!

Notes

1 Quoted in Rowan Williams, *For All That Has Been, Thanks: Growing a Sense of Gratitude*, Canterbury Press, 2010, p. 17.

2 St Augustine of Hippo, *Tractates on the Gospel of John*, tr. John Gibb. From *Nicene and Post-Nicene Fathers*, First Series, Vol. 7, Christian Literature Publishing Co., 1888.

3 Bishop John Selby Spong, *Q&A on The Parliament of the World's Religions*, weekly mailing, on www.religioustolerance.org (accessed 5 September 2007).

Notes on the 'Heart'

Throughout this book you'll find references to the 'heart'. That doesn't mean the physical, beating organ, but the centre of our being – where desires and thoughts emerge and from where we establish our identity. The 'hearth' where the Spirit kindles love and where we encounter God:

> *You shall love the Lord your God with all your heart,*
> *and with all your soul, and with all your might.*
> *Keep these words that I am commanding you today in*
> *your heart.*
> *(Deuteronomy 6.5–6)*

God also has a 'Heart' which is moved for us:

> *But Zion said, 'The Lord has forsaken me, my Lord has*
> *forgotten me.'*
> *'Can a woman forget her nursing-child,*
> *or show no compassion for the child of her womb?*
> *Even these may forget, yet I will not forget you.'*
> *(Isaiah 49.14–15)*

And God wants to renew and refresh our heart:

> *A new heart I will give you, and a new spirit I will put*
> *within you; and I will remove from your body the heart*
> *of stone and give you a heart of flesh.*
> *(Ezekiel 36.26)*

But the heart can be corrupted – can become deceitful – which is why the scriptures constantly tell us, above everything else, to guard the heart for all we do flows from it (Prov. 4.23).

> *Create a pure heart for me, O God; renew a steadfast spirit within me.*
> *(Psalm 51.10)*

Jesus recognizes the need for a 'right', renewed heart when he pronounced that those who have a pure heart will see God (Matt. 5.8). So in exploring Christian Faith it's important to remember that what we're talking about isn't a set of rules but about following Jesus who wants us to abide in his Heart (John 15.4f.) and to learn to love the world with his Sacred Heart – for ours cannot be large enough unless he dwells in them.

> *At his cross we enter the heart of the universe.*
> *All the desire wherewith he longs after a returning*
> *   sinner,*
> *makes Him esteem a broken heart ...*
> *His heart is always abroad in the midst of the earth,*
> *seeing and rejoicing in His wonders there ...*
> *   In all thy keeping, keep thy heart,*
> *   for out of it come the issues of life and death.*[1]

Note

1 Thomas Traherne (1636–74), Anglican mystic, *Centuries of Meditations*, c.1.56, 3.83, 3.88 and 4.41.

The Apostles' Creed

I believe in God,
the Father almighty, creator of heaven and earth.
I believe in Jesus Christ, his only Son, our Lord,
who was conceived by the Holy Spirit,
born of the Virgin Mary,
suffered under Pontius Pilate,
was crucified, died, and was buried;
he descended to the dead.
On the third day he rose again;
he ascended into heaven,
he is seated at the right hand of the Father,
and he will come to judge the living and the dead.
I believe in the Holy Spirit,
the holy catholic Church,
the communion of saints,
the forgiveness of sins,
the resurrection of the body,
and the life everlasting. Amen.

CREATOR

I am so plunged and submerged in the source
of his infinite love,
as if I were quite under water in the sea
and could not touch, see, feel anything on any side
except water.
St Catherine of Genoa (1447–1510)

I

Source of All Being

*Of God himself, no man can think. He may well be
loved but not thought.
By love, He may be grasped and held,
but by thought, never.*
The Cloud of Unknowing, *chapter 6*

ॐ

In the beginning

I was born just after the end of World War Two – part of
the 'baby boom' to a generation that, as Harold Macmillan
famously said, 'never had it so good'.

In many ways, mine was a typical 1950s family – a working father deeply imbued with the principles of socialism
and a stay-at-home mother who had been brought up with
Victorian notions of duty and responsibility. Father was
an agnostic Anglican bordering on atheist and Mother a
non-practising Baptist. Like many children at that time I was
sent (not taken) to Sunday school until I was nine when I
decided I didn't want to go any longer so, for the next seven
years, had nothing to do with church.

Then, at that first Midnight Mass, I sensed a door opening
onto a Presence that shook my entire being. I heard no voices,
saw no visions but just *knew* that there was something ...
something of such wonder that I was drawn into saying a
'yes' to whatever was present to me, slowly sensing that life
could never be the same again. Some can't point to any one
moment when God began to be real for them, while others

might be like those two disciples who walked along the road to Emmaus in company with a stranger until recognizing it was Jesus who journeyed with them (Luke 24.13ff.). Sometimes people travel that road for many years without seeing Jesus clearly.

> *We speak God's wisdom, secret and hidden, which God decreed before the ages for our glory. None of the rulers of this age understand this, for if they had, they would not have crucified the Lord of glory. But, as it is written,*
> *'What no eye has seen, nor ear heard,*
> *Nor the human heart conceived,*
> *What God has prepared for those who love him' –*
> *these things God has revealed to us through the Spirit; for the Spirit searches everything, even the depths of God.*
> *(1 Corinthians 2.7–10)*

Mystery, metaphor and myth

Most ancient civilizations accepted there was a prime cause for existence. While some attempted to depict the deity, Judaism, which gave birth first to Christianity and then Islam, expressly forbade making images of God (Ex. 20.4) because to do so would limit the Mystery. And Mystery, along with Metaphor and Myth, are common to all religions for they provide ways of enabling us to go beyond the world we can know through our senses to encounter what lies beyond.

Mystery is a hidden reality longing to be revealed and was, we believe, in the person of Jesus Christ. Unlike a detective 'mystery' that's got to be solved, in religious terms it concerns that which can only be revealed by God. It's not an evasion to say that God is a Mystery because, as St Ephraim the Syrian back in the fourth century realized, only something greater than God could possibly define God and there *can* be nothing greater than God. As the Little Prince in Antoine de Saint-

Exupéry's beautiful book of that name said: 'what is essential is invisible to the eye'.

Metaphor is important because it helps express matters we might 'know' but can't describe in concrete or definable ways. So when, for example, God is referred to as the 'Father almighty' it doesn't mean an actual 'father', any more than the 'heart', which we're invited to nurture, is a beating organ.

Myth is a religious account which seeks to convey a truth not dependent on facts and doesn't mean something isn't true ('oh, it's just a myth'). So, for example, when we read about Creation in Genesis (meaning 'Origins') it's a myth concerning the source of all that exists. It's not a scientific account as we might now expect in a work exploring beginnings – that's for natural scientists to debate – nor the 'how'; rather it's more about the 'why'. But more about that later.

Sadly, fundamentalists of every hue, lacking these perceptions, demand belief in a narrow, often brutal, set of rules. God is not a superstar who will solve all your problems with a click of his majestic fingers. Beware those churches which offer simple solutions to the intricate problems of life for, in claiming to be able to do so, they can be blind to the complexity of life and cause others to reject the very notion of God. Yet God does not exist – or cease to exist – according to our belief. Whether the eye of our heart is open to God or not, God *is*. We are like fish swimming through the ocean of God who is beyond every definition.

God is ... Light and Love

The problem with the thought of God as an 'almighty Father' is that it comes with so much baggage. Some may have known an abusive father; others associate God with the worst excesses of humanity – with war and violence, bigotry and persecution – which can deter us from engaging with the more important, positive dimensions of faith.

I wonder what's conjured up in your mind when you hear the word 'God'? Maybe you – like many – can't understand how a so-called loving God can allow so much suffering in the world. Some see him (and it's usually a masculine figure) as a dominant father-figure who wants to control us, or a Divine clockmaker who, having set the world in motion, is no longer interested.

But none of this was in my mind during Midnight Mass. Just a deep sense of life having meaning and purpose. That Someone – or Something – cared, and that I was embraced by arms that would draw me into a Heart that longed for me. The Heart of God. I was suddenly quite sure that God wasn't interested in whether I made a success of life, won prizes, got the top job or had the best looks. What God *was* interested in is how I *lived* … how I loved. That's the beginning of knowing 'what it's all about'.

God is love, and those who abide in love abide in God,
and God abides in them.
(1 John 4.16)

I was once asked a question about the 'Christian God' and found myself puzzled. How could there be such a thing? If God *is*, if there's anything outside human existence which cares and desires our response then he, she, it or whatever must be bigger than any faith can conceive and all those who are seeking God with all their hearts will, in the end, find they are on the same path.

God is that than which nothing greater can be thought.[1]

I like the fact that, as a catholic Christian, I am only required to say of that Being – 'I believe in one God, the Father almighty, creator of heaven and earth.' Nothing more. (I know the gender specific language will offend some but just hold on and don't let it be too distracting.)

One writer said that 'God is light and in him there is no darkness at all' (1 John 1.5) and went on to say that it's only inasmuch as we love that we will know God (1 John 4.7) and that the most important thing to realize is that we are loved in a way we can never understand.

> From Love in Love
> the leaping flame of Love is spread,
> for none can love except by Love possessed.[2]

I don't know who or what God is apart from Love (1 John 4.8) and Light (1 John 1.5). I use that capital 'L' to distinguish Divine Light from the light of the sun; a Light so bright it cannot be gazed on (Ex. 24.15f.), hidden behind a 'Cloud of Unknowing' as a medieval author named their classic book.

Divine Love differs from the emotion we experience, an emotion which reflects that Love, and which is beautifully described in one of the greatest love stories ever written: the Song of Solomon/Songs in the Old Testament. Apart from being an account of human desire it's also an allegory of Divine desire which has inspired saints to open their hearts to God. I wonder if you've ever been taken out of yourself by Love? Try it. Right at this moment, pause ... and say in the depths of your heart:

> Divine Love, I give myself to you.
> I want to know you seeping into my heart and
> embracing me

Then be quiet for a while. How do you feel? (You might call that a prayer.)

> We become what we love
> and who we love shapes what we become.
> If we love things, we become a thing.

If we love nothing, we become nothing.
Imitation is not a literal mimicking of Christ,
rather it means becoming the image of the beloved,
an image disclosed through transformation.
This means we are to become vessels of God's
compassionate love for others.[3]

God is ...

In preparing to write this book I asked a number of people what the word 'God' meant for them and here are some of their replies:

A wonderful, compassionate mysterious being,
* holding me in love.*
Limitless, undying love shining around me like a million
* suns; calling me on and on across the universe.*
A non-existent higher being or entity.
The Lover who patiently waits.
The Beginning and the End.
A sense of divine presence.
Strength in weakness.
Light in the darkness.
An ocean of Love.
A loving Father.
My mentor.
Eternal.
Creator.
Hope.

I wonder what the word conjures up for you?

All this seems somewhat unconnected with that official Christian definition of God as a Trinity of Persons – Father, Son and Holy Spirit: three equal Persons in One Being – a definition that can seem complicated. But I recall that I am (at least) three people! I was a son, I am a partner and I hope

I'm a friend. And, like the Trinity, people will experience me in different ways, yet I am just one person. Not a perfect illustration, but I hope you get my drift. The Trinity points to the way we can never exhaust our understanding of God who is beyond all names, who is the source of all life (Father), eternal Wisdom (Son) and the (Holy) Spirit of Life.

In the end, God can be no-*thing*, so although we state that God is the 'Father almighty' it doesn't mean we believe that God is a grand old man with a long white beard, but that people experience a father-like quality in the generative, divine Other.

> *Of God himself, no man can think. He may well be*
> *loved but not thought.*
> *By love, He may be grasped and held, but by thought,*
> *never.*[4]

Jesus also used another word, 'Abba' – Daddy – suggesting a far more intimate relationship. In what ways does your experience of being fathered colour your feelings about the word? Do you find it a helpful word to use when imagining God?

God as Mother

It's important to realize that God can't be identified by gender and there's a long, though not well-known, tradition of referring to God as 'Mother' some find helpful.[5]

> *Zion said, 'The Lord has forsaken me,*
> *   my Lord has forgotten me.'*
> *Can a woman forget her nursing-child,*
> *   or show no compassion for the child of her womb?*
> *Even these may forget,*
> *   yet I will not forget you.*
> *(Isaiah 49.14–15)*

In her book, *Revelations of Divine Love,* the fourteenth-century English mystic Julian of Norwich wrote extensively of the way she experienced, most particularly in Jesus, the Motherhood of God (Chapter 58ff.). References to God as Mother flowered throughout the Middle Ages in the writings, notably of the Cistercians.[6] In the end both 'father' and 'mother' indicate the source of being one might turn to – God, the source of all being enfolding all things in love.

Encountering the Other

In Islam, God has 99 'beautiful' Names which are used to describe his attributes – the All-Merciful, Compassionate, Absolute Ruler, Pure One, etc. In Judaism the 'name' is most often written as 'YHWH' which came about when Moses encountered a mysterious Other while minding sheep (Ex. 3.1–16). On just another ordinary day he had wandered with them into the wilderness where he found a flaming bush from which a voice called. When he asked who the speaker was the voice said: 'I AM WHO I AM' (Ex. 3.14) which some think is the origin of 'YHWH' (or 'Yahweh'). It could also be translated as 'I AM WHO I AM BECOMING' but it's hardly a 'name'. What do you notice about it? For me it's dynamic, creative, in process of being, never to be fully understood and forever unfolding, realized in a sudden fiery flash.

It's often in our everyday life that something occurs which opens our inner eye to a mystery that touches the soul.

> *Truly, you are a God who hides himself, O God of Israel, the Saviour.*
> *(Isaiah 45.15)*

Like others I notice that mystery in the grandeur of nature – mountains, forests, rivers and brooks; the pounding of waves against rocks; and cloud-filled skies. Many years ago, when I was walking down a lane while at St Beuno's Retreat House in North Wales, I suddenly became aware of a deep and embracing pulse of life and my inner 'spiritual eye' was awakened. I 'saw' the hedgerow and plants in a light that revealed the absolute wonder of creation. And I knew, for certain, that God is the *is-ness* of all that exists.

Such moments are a gift. But I also discover this Other in silent prayer as I open my heart to the possibility of an encounter with the One who is always present. I can be touched by the Other as I read a passage of Scripture or great poetry; listen to a Mass by Mozart or hear Plainsong; when I sing the Divine Office with those monks and nuns whose lives are given to searching for God. And I find the presence of the Divine as Mass is celebrated and the curtain separating earth from heaven momentarily drawn aside.

Lift up your hearts;
> *We lift them to the Lord.*
Let us give thanks to the Lord our God;
> *It is right to give thanks and praise ...*
> *Holy, holy, holy ...*

I encounter this presence of the Divine reaching out to me as I meditate on the life of Jesus the Christ, God's anointed One (that's what Christ means), and his saints; through those who suffer courageously and those who mourn. I have found it through being with the dying who stand at the threshold of Paradise; through kneeling before Christ present in the Blessed Sacrament as it is enthroned before our gaze on an altar. I encounter the Divine through the Beatitudes which invite me to live beyond the confines of my, oh so often, narrow self. And I find it in the arms of him who loves me.

But there are those who look at mountains and see only rocks or listen to Mozart and hear only notes. Yet everything is touched with the Divine.

You ask,
'Prove God exists.'

I ask,
where is the home of love,
the storehouse of beauty
or the source of music which moves the heart?

Tell me
where I can find the spring of joy
or the heart of wonder?

Show me
where is the fountain of compassion;
where mercy and pity live.

God is –
in the air I breathe,
the earth I touch,
the sea in which I swim.

God is –
that ocean of life
in whom we live and move and have our being,
whose offspring I am and without whom I cannot exist;
the One who is and was and ever shall be.

God is all that is most noble
seeking the nobility in me.
All that you and I can be
as we say our 'yes' to that call.

What need I prove
– only that I am not deaf to that call;
or blind to that sight?

Invitation:

Enlivened by the 'breath' of God, spend some moments consciously focusing into your breath. Slowly inhale and exhale and be aware of the breath entering deeply into your lungs.

Notes

1 St Anselm, *Proslogion* (1078), St Augustine's Press, 2013.
2 Fr Gilbert Shaw, by kindness of the Sisters of the Love of God.
3 St Clare of Assisi (1194–1253).
4 *The Cloud of Unknowing* (author unknown, fourteenth century), Penguin Classics, 2001, ch. 6.
5 See also Vatican website: www.vatican.va/spirit/documents/spirit_20010807_giuliana-norwich_en.html
6 Caroline Walker Bynum, *Jesus as Mother: Studies in the Spirituality of the High Middle Ages*, Center for Medieval and Renaissance Studies, UCLA, 1984.

2

Creator of Heaven and Earth

The glory of God is a living man; and the life of man
consists in beholding God.
St Irenaeus, Against Heresies, Book 4, 20:7

ॐ

Have you ever gone out into a starlit night, looked up into the heavens and wondered at the marvel of it all? When I began testing my vocation to the Anglican Franciscans (the Society of St Francis) at Hilfield Friary in Dorset I'd often walk, after Compline, to the bottom of the great avenue of lime trees leading to the cemetery, rest my arms on the gate and look up at the glorious canopy of the Milky Way. The silence of the night was pervading, but so was its sheer majesty. If you've never done that, try opening yourself to the immensity of space and contemplate this vast mystery in which we exist and let it speak to you.

Many say that science has 'disproved' the existence of God, but does the existence of God lie in the domain of science as we understand that word? God lies beyond definition because the term involves eternity and infinity and any reality beyond that.

This also is Thou; neither is this Thou.
(Ancient saying)

Being in the presence of the material wonders of creation – a star-studded sky, immense oceans or majestic mountains – can evoke a sense of awe and wonder. Yet some, seeing so

much injustice, pain and suffering, decide that if God does
exist then 'he' must be very evil to have created such monstrous things. But recognizing such complexity, Christianity
knows that 'evil' must coexist with 'good'; what appear to
be random, sometimes chaotic processes are indispensable if
we're to have the universe we know (and we can't know any
other). If things had been even slightly different, life probably
couldn't have emerged from primordial chaos. And still the
world is alive and active – earthquakes, tsunamis, hurricanes
– all aspects of a living planet as much as autumnal leaves,
waterfalls and gentle breezes. So as we look at the Universe
and are moved by awe and wonder we're taken beyond
science into the realm of the spiritual:

> *When I see the heavens, the work of your fingers,*
> *the moon and the stars which you arranged,*
> *what is man that you should keep him in mind,*
> *the son of man that you care for him?*
> *(Psalm 8.3–4)*

This isn't about 'creationism', the belief that everything came
into being literally as Genesis said. Such literalism might
appeal to fundamentalists, but it misses the point, and the
point is that the heart of Creation is Godly and good, infused
with divine beauty.

Christian ecology

Anyone reading the opening chapter of the first book of
the Bible can't help but notice the way it's almost a song of
creation with its repeated line: 'God said, "Let there be ..."
And there was' and its refrain: 'And God saw that it was
good.' Perhaps that notion led the devout Roman Catholic
writer J. R. R. Tolkien to describe in *The Silmarillion* the way
the world was 'sung' into existence (p. 15), a notion reflected

in the Preface of the Church of England's Eucharistic Prayer G:

From the beginning you have created all things
and all your works echo the silent music of your praise.

The Psalms also frequently refer to this 'music' of creation:

Before you all the earth shall bow down,
shall sing to you, sing to your name!
(Psalm 66.4)

What's clear is that Creation was intended to exist in harmony with its Creator. Back in the twelfth century St Francis of Assisi (Patron Saint of Ecology), realizing the interrelatedness of all things, celebrated this in his *Canticle of Creation*. In it he referred to the moon, fire and water, the wolf and ass – even death itself – as brother and sister under God our 'Father' and Earth our 'Mother'. We're one with creation which originated in the sacred mystery – the Heart – of Being. Francis realized that this creation came into being as the overflow of Divine Love, meaning that we need to be involved in caring for the environment.

What (Christians) need is an 'ecological conversion',
whereby the effects of their encounter with Jesus Christ
become evident in their relationship with the world
around them. Living our vocation to be protectors
of God's handiwork is essential to a life of virtue; it is
not an optional or a secondary aspect of our Christian
experience.[1]

In the image of God

Christianity affirms the creative, loving heart of God who brought into existence worlds both material *and* spiritual – angels and archangels and all the spiritual beings attendant on God (Rev. 4.6ff.) with whom we join in worship. Yet *you* are the greatest wonder of all creation, the 'crown' of God's works:

> God created humankind in his image,
> in the image of God he created them;
> male and female he created them.
> *(Genesis 1.27)*

It doesn't matter what your gender, ethnicity or sexuality (it's tragic that some Christians still think gay sex is sinful), you're beautiful to God. The wonder of our being is that we bear, deep within us, the Divine image; not an image as in a photograph but the imprint of a loving God to *be love* in the world. At *heart* we find original blessing not original sin and need to reject any notion that we are 'utterly depraved' or 'sinners in the hands of an angry god'. Genesis 1.31 says that God looked upon the whole of creation and found it 'very good' and that doesn't change: despite our failures, God sees into the deepest place within our heart and finds there the Divine image.

Christianity says that being made in the 'image' of God we have about us, in the deepest part of our being, the potential for greatness, beauty and wonder. For holiness. I can love and value myself because God does. Just consider that for a moment – doesn't it take your breath away?

Original Sin

But then there's that matter of the apple and the serpent (Gen. 3). Poor Eve, the 'mother of all the living' ('Adam' means 'of the earth'), gets a bad press but this isn't the place to explore issues of patriarchy which lie behind much of the Old Testament. The account of how humankind, created to live in harmony with its Creator, was barred from the Paradise of Eden gives us the teaching about Original Sin and shows how humankind seems prone to the attraction of 'evil'. Yet there remains, deep within us, a desire to return to our Original Innocence and at-one-ness with God. The problem of creating anything and giving it the gift of freedom is that you can't control what it then does – and the greater the possibility for good the greater, alas, the possibility of its darker, shadow side (evil) emerging into the world.

Trying to make an earthly paradise, we often forget that can only be done in union with the Creator with whom the divine image within us longs for deeper union. Within the heart there's a desire for at-one-ness with God longing to express itself, wanting to be captured by the One who is Love and Life who never ceases to desire to enfold us into the paradise of Divine union, no matter how long that might take:

> *Late have I loved you,*
> *O Beauty ever ancient, ever new,*
> *late have I loved you!*
> *You were within me, but I was outside,*
> *and it was there that I searched for you.*
> *In my unloveliness I plunged into the lovely things*
>   *which you created.*
> *You were with me, but I was not with you.*
> *Created things kept me from you;*
> *yet if they had not been in you they would have not been*
>   *at all.*

You called, you shouted, and you broke through my
   deafness.
You flashed, you shone, and you dispelled my blindness.
You breathed your fragrance on me;
I drew in breath and now I pant for you.
I have tasted you, now I hunger and thirst for more.
You touched me, and I burned for your peace.[2]

Close your eyes. In a minute of silence, consider: 'I am made in the image of God – the image of divine beauty which is so much deeper than the eye can see. I have the potential to be – Godlike.' Just be quiet and mull over that.

ॐ

The call to holiness and the gods of our age

Our early ancestors were nomads, hunter-gatherers before they were settlers, and that memory is in our DNA. It finds expression through the need for pilgrimage – we are pilgrims in search of that which will satisfy our deepest cravings, yet some give up attending to this need. No wonder secular society can feel lost and people look for someone to lead them to seemingly brighter pastures. 'God, you have made us for yourself, and our hearts are restless till they find their rest in you', wrote St Augustine. Recognizing the importance of holy places, Christianity encourages us to move from the known to the unknown, to be pilgrims given to the heart's search for God, the source of all being.

Yet despite this amazing affirmation made by our Faith, the appeal of other gods – those of power and wealth, beauty and celebrity – to satisfy our needs blinds many. Going to church has been replaced by the weekly visit to the shopping mall – you arrive at the awe-inspiring entrance and move into another world with its 'chancel' (the atrium), 'side chapels' (branches of national chains) and a 'sanctuary' containing the shrine to a major supermarket. But does all that *really* satisfy? In an age when nail bars and fake tan shops fill the high street, can our hopes and dreams be really satisfied by shopping or attempts to stay young and beautiful?

> *Rouse yourself, man, and recognize the dignity of your nature. Remember that you were made in God's image; though corrupted in Adam, that image has been restored in Christ. Use creatures as they should be used: the earth, the sea, the sky, the air, the springs and the rivers. Give praise and glory to their Creator for all that you find beautiful and wonderful in them. See with your bodily eyes the light that shines on earth, but embrace with your whole soul and all your affections the true light which enlightens every man who comes into this world.*[3]

We know the dangers of becoming addicted to smart phones and losing the ability to connect with the world around us or becoming enticed by celebrities, forgetting that we are but dust – of the earth – though dust destined for glory. Capable of the greatest acts of kindness, generosity, selflessness and creativity we're also capable of their opposite, and that capacity for ill needs overcoming by attending to the good. The wonders of which we're capable have, over centuries, been attributed to God and, affirming that we have the image of God within us, saints like Francis of Assisi, Charles de Foucauld, Teresa of Calcutta and myriad others have striven to incarnate God's grace in their lives.

The power of the opposite to truth, beauty and goodness has also been recognized and named as evil. Yet as Western society rejects, denies or ignores the notion of God and Godliness, so those dark, corrupting forces continue to catch people's attention, working on our imagination and seeming to be more real than any source of goodness.

Dictators and demagogues

But when the God of life and love is ignored, that space can fill with other gods and some can be quite nasty. Demagogues and dictators – secular or religious – working on our fears offer security and certainty and the appeal of nationalism can take over when the Christian understanding of our common humanity is lost. We begin to retreat behind barriers rather than learning how to reach out to the other who requires respect because they, too, are made in God's likeness. That's what makes Jesus' parable of the Good Samaritan so shocking (Luke 10.25–37) and why the story of God coming among us in Jesus is such a countercultural narrative.

Into this condition those words of St Leo echo: 'Rouse yourself, man, and recognize the dignity of your nature.' I wonder if we've forgotten that? Forgotten that dignity needs working at because it's easy to fall victim to hatred and violence – physical, emotional or spiritual; easy to fall victim to self-hatred. Ours is an age which needs saints – women and men who place a premium on living out of our human worth; who are prepared to spend time and energy cultivating a relationship with God and goodness in their lives; who hear the call to live out of our blessedness rather than our selfishness.

The Mystery of the Trinity

Ultimately God is a Mystery which Christianity speaks of as a Trinity of Persons – Father, Son and Holy Spirit (or Creator, Redeemer and Sanctifier) – in one Being. And if that sounds odd then just consider that there are many 'persons' in you: you're a different person in the eyes of your parent(s), your partner (if you have one) and your friends, and the task of each of us is to somehow hold these different 'persons' together.

This union of Persons is close to the Sufi understanding of God as 'Oneness of Being', what I term the Sacred Heart of Being. Whatever God 'is' all we can do is to 'stand under' – gaze upon or contemplate – rather than 'understand' this mystery.

God himself is the Word that cannot be uttered,
and himself the Word that speaks to all.[4]

That 'Sacred Heart of Being' is what birthed the sun, moon and stars and from that Oneness the whole of creation flows. There's an icon (a painting with hidden meaning) of the Trinity by Andre Rublev, a fourteenth-century Russian artist, which many find expresses this mystery in a unique way. It shows three seated Beings gazing upon each other with eyes of compassionate love in which the beholder is held:

When all the words to speak of God have been exhausted it's in silence that we're most present to this sacred Heart of Being which isn't far from us but is as close to us as our breath. And, through the breath of God, Jesus came among us to draw us back into our primal union. This is the first Mystery of Faith

❧

O God,
held in the palm of your hand,
I thank you for the wonder of my being,
May I know you in the depths of my heart
and lovingly call out to you from its silence;
may I seek you in and through your Creation
and may my life be a song of praise to you,
Creator, Redeemer and Sanctifier.
Amen.

❧

Invitation:

Go for a walk and, one by one, allow all your senses to engage with the world. See, hear, smell, etc. ... the world around you. Realize yourself connected with creation and thank God for each experience.

Notes

1 *Laudato Si.* 217 © Libreria Editrice Vaticana.
2 St Augustine of Hippo, *Confessions* 10:27.
3 St Leo the Great (400–461), Nativitate Domini: Sermo 7.
4 *Sant Kabir, Mira Bai, Shaikh Farid, Bhikan and Surdas,* ch. 9, ed. O. P. Ralhan, Anmol Publications, New Delhi, 1997.

Chapters 1 and 2

For reflection and discussion

- Who is God for you?
- In what ways are you taken out of yourself? How does that make you feel? What 'name' might *you* give to God?
- What does being 'made in the image of God' say to you?
- How might Genesis inform a Christian's approach to caring for the planet?
- How does your lifestyle impact the environment?
- What response might you make to the thought that God has been searching for you since you were born (Ps. 139)?

REDEEMER

In the first creation God gave me myself;
but in his new creation he gave me himself,
and by that gift restored to me the self that I had lost.
St Bernard of Clairvaux (1090–1153)
On Loving God, Chapter 5

3

The Image of the Invisible One

He belongs to you, but more than that,
He longs to be in you,
living and ruling in you, as the head lives
and rules in the body.
He wants His breath to be in your breath,
His heart in your heart, and His soul in your soul.
St John Eudes (1601–80)

ॐ

At first, Christ didn't mean as much to me as a general sense that God was a reality to which I wanted to respond. It's not that Jesus wasn't there, just that I found the way some Christians talked about him rather off-putting, and I didn't share their experience of being 'saved'. But, slowly, I began to connect with him and when, in my twenties, I encountered St Francis I realized the difference Jesus could make. Francis' deep devotion to Jesus touched me, not least when I discovered he'd created the first Christmas Crib at Greccio in Italy to help people realize that God loves us so much that he entered the flesh of a baby in a nondescript village called Bethlehem, a birth that connects God with suffering humanity right from the start.

God *choosing* to be born into the family of a carpenter who'd been forced by the government to leave home, who couldn't find decent accommodation when his wife went into labour and who, with her and their child, had to flee his homeland, has been seen as the way God has a 'preferential option for the poor'.[1] Yet all that can mean nothing unless we allow God to be born into our heart – today.

Luke records that birth in his Gospel (which means 'good news') giving us all the details that make Christmas special – shepherds and angels, Mary and Joseph sheltering in a stable and Jesus in the manger (Luke 2). Matthew mentions its occurrence; Mark simply begins with Jesus' baptism when he was about 30 and John – well, John takes a completely different approach. For him what mattered was that in Jesus we encounter God, so began from a different perspective:

> *In the beginning was the Word,*
> *and the Word was with God,*
> *and the Word was God ...*
> *And the Word became flesh and lived among us*
> *and we have seen his glory, the glory as of a father's*
>   *only son.*
> *(John 1.1, 14)*

Seeing God in Christ

For Orthodox Christians it's 'seeing' the glory that matters. For them the Epiphany – the 'showing forth' to the Magi – was more important, for it was strangers from abroad who first recognized this manifestation of God (Matt. 2). A manifestation that was declared in the Baptism of Jesus and then through the first miracle at Cana in Galilee when water was changed into wine.

Jesus, the 'Word' of the Father

St John saw that glory – that God was enfleshed (what's called 'Incarnation') – and 'seeing' this mystery with the eye of the heart he wants us all to come to 'believe' that Jesus is the Father's Son, that 'through believing (we) might have life ...'

(John 20.31). God can be seen and touched in a human being whose existence isn't just recorded in the Gospels but also by the first-century Jewish and Roman historians Josephus and Tacitus. Jesus reveals the nature of God; who God is we see in Jesus, the 'lens' through which we then need to read the Scriptures.

John recounts a number of 'signs' which reveal the glory of God in this Man – water changed to wine (2.1–11), loaves multiplied (6.1–14), blindness healed (9.1ff.), etc. Many are linked to 'I am' statements – 'the bread of life', 'the Light of the world'. Faith, for John, can never be separated from matter – human matter – bodies and blood, sweat and, eventually, a crucified God reigning from a tree, and if you can *see* that with the eye of your heart you'll come to believe.

So, John begins his Gospel with that astounding claim: 'The Word became flesh' – no sweet and homely account of the birth of the baby Jesus for him, rather an affirmation that God has taken on our flesh, entered our bloodstream and, shockingly, in Christ will be crucified. For him this was what he wanted people to grasp: God doesn't just want to make us good or more moral, but to share his life with us – enable us to enter *his* life.

You'd have thought John might have made it a little easier and begun by telling us some practical things about Jesus. Instead he says that Jesus was the 'Word' and, in doing so, echoes the opening of Genesis:

> *In the beginning when God created the heavens and the earth, the earth was a formless void and darkness covered the face of the deep, while a wind from God swept over the face of the waters. Then God said, 'Let there be light'; and there was light.*

This 'Word' is 'life' and 'light' (John 1.4) straightway linking this beginning with God's first creation.

Seeing and believing

It may seem an odd way to introduce John's readers to Jesus – but we all come to him by different paths. My own introduction was through the mystery of the Mass and this sense of being held in a Divine otherness (transcendence). It took me time to discover the 'immanence' of God in Christ – that all the glory I sensed around me was focused in Him.

I first came to a deeper encounter with Jesus when I was about 17 and had started going to a church in the City of London where, opposite the entrance, stood a life-sized crucifix.[2] Here I experienced my second revelation because as I stood looking at the figure I suddenly thought: if the Son of God loved people so much that he suffered and died for them then this is the most important thing I've got to understand and life cannot be the same again. The 'word' I heard as I gazed on him there, hanging on the cross, was 'I love you *this* much.'

Fifty and more years have passed and my conversion – the conversion of my heart – is ongoing. Some may be able to point to a moment when they made a decisive decision but that mustn't be used as a badge of belonging making others feel they're not 'real' Christians. Those who have had such an experience need to exercise humility: what matters is not how you *came* to faith but how you *live* it. Our hearts have to be constantly converted to the love of God.

Christ is the 'image' of God

St Paul also talked about Jesus as the 'image of the invisible God' and went on to write of him as the 'firstborn of all creation', the cause of all that is – visible and invisible – in whom the 'fullness of God' dwells, whose coming was to reconcile all things (Col. 1.15–22).

This enfleshment of God is the wonder of our Faith. Jesus is both fully human *and* fully Divine. And because Jesus is the 'image' of God the early Church decided that, despite a prohibition in the Ten Commandments against the worship of 'idols' (Ex. 20.4), it is quite permissible to make images of Jesus and the saints – necessary, in fact. Because if God chose to reveal invisible things in visible matter then we honour God by doing the same.

The very best thing one can ever do is to fix Jesus in one's heart and never want anything else.[3]

Yet more wonderful still, I began to realize that what I see in him is a bright reflection of what lies within me. I can reflect aspects of that diamond-studded Divine compassion and love that dwells in him; my being contains a reflection of the wonder he incarnated which we can all reveal. If you behold glory in the Child of Bethlehem, that glory can be reflected in you.

If you've sensed the 'aroma' of God then let it draw you to seek to explore your own depths, the ground of your existence. And that depth plunges into a great silence where God's Word silently echoes in the heart; the enlightening silence of love.

*If the baby in the manger distracts you
from seeing what lies in the cave of Bethlehem,
that reflection of the depth of human life,*

then look beyond and realize the potential present
  in yourself,
the mystery that lies in the recesses of your own heart.
Perhaps the importance of this Feast isn't just that we
  celebrate God's incarnation
it's that we find hope for ourselves and the world.

෴

Invitation:

Slowly read the sayings of Jesus (Chapter 5a) and notice which 'speaks' to you. Let the words sink into your heart and read them again. Look up the saying in a Bible and notice its context. What might Jesus be saying to you? Speak to him about what you notice. Who can you share this with?

Notes

1 Pope Francis, *Evangelii gaudium*, Veritas, 2013, pp. 186–216.
2 A crucifix is a cross bearing the figure of Jesus crucified.
3 Richard Rolle, *The Fire of Love* (late fourteenth century), Penguin Classics, 1981.

4

Son of a Virgin

Never be afraid of loving the Blessed Virgin too much.
You can never love her more than Jesus did.
St Maximilian Kolbe (1894–1941)

❧

What makes Christianity different from other major religions is in claiming that God wasn't just revealed among us, but chose to be born of an earthly woman, one who has ever since been called Blessed. Who gave herself, body and soul, to her Creator.

Back in the twelfth century St Hildegard of Bingen, the great German mystic, exclaimed that she was 'a feather on the breath of God ...' That seems a perfect description of what we know of the one chosen *by* God (Luke 1.26–38) and reflects what our relationship with God might become. Mary uniquely lived out of the Divine Will and her heart must have been pure enough to act as God's dwelling-place, for would God have chosen a broken vessel to bring about the Incarnation? If you wanted to entrust yourself into someone's hands wouldn't you be *very* careful whom you chose?

Mary the dawn, Christ the perfect Day;
Mary the Gate, Christ the Heav'nly Way;
Mary the Temple, Christ the Temple's Lord;
Mary the Shrine, Christ the God adored.[1]

Full of grace

Only a good tree, Jesus observed, can produce good fruit (Matt. 7.17) which leads to an understanding that Mary's heart was completely given to God for the sake of the fruit of her womb. She would have been familiar with the beautiful love poem known as the Song of Songs/Solomon read at every Passover and often at other times in Jewish households and would have known about the desire of the bride for the Bridegroom, or the soul for God:

> *You have ravished my heart, my sister, my bride,*
> *you have ravished my heart with a glance of your eyes.*
> *(4.9a)*

Mary, knowing herself loved by God, abandoned herself *to* God and was filled with grace. It may seem strange to spend time talking about Mary as we reflect on Jesus but just as the 'breath' of God brought about the first Creation (Gen. 1.2) so the Holy Spirit 'overshadowed' Mary at the Annunciation to bring about this new creation. And if ever you visit an Orthodox church you'll find that right at the centre of the great icon screen (*iconostasis*) which hides the sanctuary from the rest of the church are two doors, the Holy or Royal Doors through which Word and Sacrament come forth and on which are shown the Archangel Gabriel and Mary at the Annunciation, powerfully reminding us that we owe our Faith to her 'fiat' – her 'let it be to me'.

The New Eve

Just as Jesus is the 'New Adam' so Mary is the 'New Eve' whose fiat reversed the effects of Eve's disobedience.

(The Son of God) became man through the Virgin that the disobedience caused by the serpent might be destroyed in the same way in which it had originated. For Eve, while a virgin incorrupt, conceived the word which proceeded from the serpent, and brought forth disobedience and death. But the Virgin Mary was filled with faith and joy when the Angel Gabriel told her the glad tidings ... And through her was he born ...[2]

I know someone who, having left the Christianity of their childhood, became involved with different forms of spirituality until, eventually, she encountered Mary in a dream and was led back to Christ. Mary enables us to touch the divine feminine that is in all of us, yet which can be lost if she is not given a place in our Faith. She is the one to whom we can confide our cares and concerns and ask for help in growing closer to her Son – to have a share in her heart's love for him.

Let it be with me

Mary was a woman who listened, deep within her, to God's call. A human being who co-operated with the Holy Spirit in this work of new creation: 'Let it be with me according to your word' (Luke 1.38b). On the back wall of our garden at home hangs a plaque of the Annunciation and I sometimes sit looking at it wondering what God might be saying to me – am I listening in the silence of *my* heart? Can I trust God enough to say those words?

Bend my heart to your will, O God.
(cf. Psalm 119.36)

Mother of God

Isn't it amazing that a woman lies at the heart of our Faith! She brings a feminine touch to the story and to our encounter with God; a young woman ('virgin') co-operates with God and gives birth to a Child. She is blessed because she listened to the word of God and kept it (Luke 11.28). We, who hear and keep that Word, are his Mother bearing Christ in the womb of our heart and giving birth to him in our actions.

> *Mary heard God's word and kept it, and so she is blessed. She kept God's truth in her mind, a nobler thing than carrying his body in her womb.*[3]

In listening to God in the depths of her heart where Jesus was conceived, Mary shows an example of the contemplative life. What is a 'contemplative'? Someone who takes a long, attentive and loving look at life – at God. In an age of activism, often animated by dark forces, we need to develop this contemplative dimension: God invites us to nurture a contemplative heart rooted in silence and stillness and focused on faith, hope and love. Action needs to emerge from contemplation (just imagine the difference it might make if, before any vote in Parliament, our MPs had to spend ten minutes in silence...). Mary spent time pondering Gabriel's message before responding (Luke 1.29); being needs to precede doing for true transformation – rooted in the conversion of the heart – to occur.

Jesus and Mary have always belonged together and when, in the early Christian era, disputes raged as to his nature it was to Mary that Christians turned for an answer. The fact that she bore a child both human and Divine led to her being called *Theotokos* – Mother of God – thus safeguarding our Faith.

In the end you can't love Mary more than her Son did and, like many sons, Jesus must delight in his Mother being praised and honoured, and grieve when she is ignored or abused.

The Sorrowful Mother

The life of Mary shows us that, even though chosen by God, that didn't stop her experiencing suffering. While there were times of profound joy (the Annunciation, Incarnation, Adoration of the Kings, Resurrection and Ascension of her Son and her entrance into Heaven) these are countered with times of profound sorrow. There are 'Seven Sorrows' she particularly faced: being told she would experience deep suffering (Luke 2.34–35); having to flee with her husband and child as refugees (Matt. 2.13); losing her child (Luke 2.43–51); meeting her Son as he was led to death; being at his crucifixion (John 19.25); receiving her dead son – she is often shown bearing the body of Jesus in her lap after he was taken down from the cross, and attending his burial (John 19.40–42).

Mary is a mother we can turn to at moments of agonizing grief and pain. Her life shows us that even the Mother of God was not saved from sorrow, not spared from knowing the depths of misery, just as God didn't spare himself.

The Blessed Virgin

Some think that because the Gospels refer to Jesus' 'brothers and sisters' she must have had other children. But if Mary *had* borne other children, why was it necessary for Jesus to commit her to John at the Crucifixion (John 19.25)? Rather, in the Middle East, where I used to travel, it's still quite common to refer to cousins in that way – the nuclear family is a very modern, Western notion.

So we celebrate her with statues and icons before which millions are drawn to light candles as they, too, come before this mystery: that, for nine months, God was held in the womb of a woman filled with grace. A mother whose love for her Son can teach us about intimacy with him if we open our heart. A woman whose profound 'let it be to me' teaches all her children to place their faith in Jesus.

The Angelus

St Francis of Assisi had a deep love of Mary and the Incarnation, so when he first encountered Muslims and their call to prayer five times a day it's thought he encouraged the devotion we refer to as the Angelus. He certainly wanted to encourage ordinary people to pray each day and by 1269 St Bonaventure tells the Friars to teach people to pray the Angelus three times a day in honour of the Word becoming flesh. Today a bell is often rung in the early morning, at noon and in the evening – our call to prayer – reminding us of our Faith and rooting us in prayer.

The Angelus

The Angel of the Lord brought tidings to Mary,
And she conceived of the Holy Spirit.

Hail Mary, full of grace, the Lord is with thee,
blessed art thou among women,
and blessed is the fruit of thy womb, Jesus.
Holy Mary, Mother of God, pray for us sinners,
now and at the hour of our death. Amen

Behold the handmaid of the Lord.
Let it be to me according to thy Word.
Hail Mary, etc. ...

And the Word was made flesh,
And dwelt among us.
Hail Mary, etc. ...

Pray for us, O holy Mother of God.
That we may be made worthy of the promises of Christ.

Let us pray:
We beseech thee, O Lord,
pour thy grace into our hearts;
that as we have known the incarnation of thy Son,
    Jesus Christ,
by the message of an angel, so by His cross and passion
we may be brought to the glory of his Resurrection.
Through the same Christ, our Lord. *Amen.*

☙

Invitation:

Slowly read Luke 1.26–38. Relish each word and phrase and
notice if any stand out for you. Then stop. Slowly read it
again – let it sink deeper into your heart and notice, again,
what stands out. Hold that and let it sink even deeper. Try
expressing what you've discovered and then be quiet and
sense if there's any movement in your own heart. Finally, sit
in silence for a few minutes.

Notes

1 Traditional.

2 St Justin Martyr (d. 165), *Dialogue with Trypho*, ch. 100, *Patro-logia Graeca (PG)*, Migne, 6, pp. 709–12.

3 St Augustine, *Sermons on selected lessons of the New Testament*, Sermon 25, 7–8, PL 46, pp. 937–8.

5

As One Who Serves

*Let your way of life among the people be such
that whoever sees or hears you will glorify
and praise your heavenly Father.*
St Francis of Assisi

༝

You are my Beloved Son

Along with the Creed the Gospels are also silent about Jesus'
early life and ministry. His first 30 years are hidden from us
until the day when he approaches his cousin, John, at the
river Jordan (Matt. 3). John was baptizing people as a sign of
their beginning a new life: don't let greed rule you, share with
the poor, stop telling lies – for the reign of God is about to
begin. And he's accusing the Jewish leaders of being a 'brood
of snakes', which angered them but played well with ordinary
folk.

It's in this disturbing context he baptizes Jesus by plunging
him beneath the waters. As he emerges, 'suddenly the heavens
were opened to him and he saw the Spirit of God descending
like a dove and alighting on him. And a voice from heaven
said, "This is my Son, the Beloved, with whom I am well
pleased"' (Matt. 3.16–17). It was a moment of profound
revelation; and we need to know the words Jesus heard are
also spoken to us – *you* are my beloved daughter, my beloved
son. And when we hear *that* deep in our hearts, then we can
move on. 'And the Spirit immediately drove him into the
wilderness' (Mark 1.12).

The Temptations

'He was in the wilderness for forty days, tempted by Satan' (Mark 1.13). In the prime of his life (it's thought most people then only lived until 35–40), those days are recorded by Matthew, Mark and Luke. What they're clear about is that, as he fasted, he was tested. In that place of solitude he faced his own demons which tempted him in those areas of life in which he needed to be strong. He, like many of us, had to face the lure of materialism, the lust for power and the need to be sure he trusted God. Imitating Jesus, Christians often spend time in 'retreat' when, apart from anything else, they can face, in solitude, what's driving them.

This wilderness time is also recalled through Lent. It can be an exercise in restraint – giving up chocolate, for example – or a time when we struggle with our deeper desires, when our calling is challenged. We all have temptations that test our identity; Jesus faced his own, what might yours be? There will be another time, later on, in a garden at night, when he will again be put to the test but, for now, Jesus is ready to begin the next phase and moves back to Galilee.

Life in the Beatitudes

For the next three years he will live in the northern region of Israel where most of his ministry takes place. He had come to know some of those who fished on the inland Sea of Galilee and four of them became his first disciples – Andrew, Simon Peter, James and his brother John. It's a region far from Jerusalem, the turbulent political and religious capital, and all the Gospels contain stories of the healing, miracles and teaching that, over a period of just three years, occurred here.

At the start, Jesus condensed much of his teaching into what we call the Beatitudes:

*Blessed are the poor in spirit, for theirs is the kingdom
of heaven.*
Blessed are those who mourn, for they will be comforted.
Blessed are the meek, for they will inherit the earth.
*Blessed are those who hunger and thirst for
righteousness, for they will be filled.*
Blessed are the merciful, for they will receive mercy.
Blessed are the pure in heart, for they will see God.
*Blessed are the peacemakers, for they will be called
children of God.*
*Blessed are those who are persecuted for righteousness'
sake,*
for theirs is the kingdom of heaven.
*Blessed are you when people revile you and persecute you
and utter all kinds of evil against you falsely on my
account.*
Rejoice and be glad, for your reward is great in heaven,
*for in the same way they persecuted the prophets who
were before you.*
(Matthew 5.3–11)

Jesus is saying that 'blessedness', a word meaning being
'on the right track', comes from seeking to live out of these
sayings because then you're fulfilling God's Will. Unique
to Christianity, they're seen as Jesus' response to the Ten
Commandments (Ex. 20.2–17), except these are not Laws
but sources of blessing giving us an insight into how the
Divine Will works.

Teaching

Jesus was known as a rabbi, a Jewish teacher (Mark 9.5),
who often taught using parables – word-pictures inviting
imaginative responses. I wonder if you realize how much some
of these have influenced our culture? Here are a few examples:

- Our neighbour isn't just the person who lives next door but anyone for whom we need to act as a 'good Samaritan'. And as Jews hated Samaritans this is also an important lesson about how we regard 'foreigners' and what they can often teach us (Luke 10.25–37).
- Giving people another chance if they ask for it reflects the account of the 'Prodigal Son' who, having acquired everything he wanted, squanders his inheritance before returning to his father asking for forgiveness and to be allowed home (Luke 15.11–24).
- Fear can lead us to 'bury our talents' (Matt. 25.14–30).
- Wealth mustn't blind us to the needs of the poor (Luke 16.19–31).

People grappled with these word-pictures and Jesus often used them to denounce the corruption of those in power. In Matthew's Gospel he calls the religious leaders of his day 'blind guides' (15.14); 'hypocrites' who look good on the outside but are full of corruption (23.27). In a small society he gradually stirred up a lot of anger among the powerful, accusing them of being more interested in making money than exercising justice and mercy (23.23).

Miracles and healings

You might know stories about healings performed by Jesus – the blind see (Mark 8.22–26), lepers are made whole (Matt. 8.1–4), a paralysed man walks (Luke 5.17–26) and many others – but they're not just recorded to show Jesus as a miracle worker. There are other layers to these accounts – Jesus has power over nature, connects with the outcast, is able to free people from what prevents them living life more fully and is more interested in our well-being than keeping the rules.

Liberating

All this was happening against a background of Roman occupation; many were looking for a leader in whom they could put their trust and who would liberate them. Gradually some began to see Jesus as such a figure because he was doing many of the things that prophets do – challenging authority, calling people back to God, spending time in the desert. He was clearly not a 'one-off' because he had a growing group of followers. Was he the Messiah, the one whom people believed would come and make Israel great again? The saviour of the people?

Jesus avoided this label, especially when it became clear that one of his disciples, Peter, was beginning to think he might be (Matt. 16.23). So imagine Peter's shock when Jesus said to him:

> *'If any want to become my followers, let them deny themselves and take up their cross and follow me. For those who want to save their life will lose it, and those who lose their life for my sake will find it. For what will it profit them if they gain the whole world but forfeit their life? Or what will they give in return for their life?'*
> *(Matthew 16.24–26)*

Transfigured by glory

The turning point seems to have occurred at his Transfiguration (Matt. 17.1–8) after which the road to the cross began. Jesus, along with Peter, James and John, climbed a 'high mountain' and was enveloped in a cloud, just as had happened to Moses on Mount Sinai (Ex. 19.16ff.).

Throughout the Scriptures there are epiphanies – moments when something is revealed. Often we can't see beyond the surface of life: 'now we see in a mirror, dimly,' St Paul wrote

(1 Cor. 13.12) but there will come a time when 'we will see face to face. Now I know only in part; then I will know fully, even as I have been fully known.' What does that say to you?

In Jesus we see something of the glory of God – a foretaste of resurrection – and as we encounter him, have the potential to be changed: to be, as St Paul wrote: 'transformed into the same image from one degree of glory to another; for this comes from the Lord, the Spirit' (2 Cor. 3.18). To look on the face of Jesus is to see something of the glory of God, the embrace of whose Love is enlightening. By turning our faces to Christ, we desire to be filled with the life of God. Isn't that what lovers want to do: give life to each other?

When Jesus reached the summit of this mountain, he had a profound experience of Divine overshadowing and was transfigured, enlightened as he heard the words: 'This is my Son, the Beloved.' Again, we're invited to hear, deep in our hearts, those words – 'You are my beloved' – and to believe it. *Every* part of you, no matter your gender, sexuality, ability, ethnicity, religion and so on, is beloved by God.

Jesus,
your heart went out to those who suffered:
the lost, those bound by sin
and those longing for life.
Help us with your grace and mercy
that we might take up our cross each day
and follow you.

છે

Invitation:

Read John 4.5–15. Close your eyes and imagine a well in your heart descending into rivers of life. Notice what lies in the depths of that well and any feelings that emerge. Turn your gaze on Jesus who sits with you beside that well and share any of this with him.

5a

Jesus Said

Read the following verses and notice which 'speaks' to you. Let the words sink into your heart. Look up the saying in a Bible and notice its context. What might Jesus be saying to you? If you can, talk about this in a group or with your priest.

'There is nothing outside a person that by going in can defile, but the things that come out are what defile.'
(Mark 7.15)

'If any want to become my followers, let them deny themselves and take up their cross and follow me. For those who want to save their life will lose it, and those who lose their life for my sake, and for the sake of the gospel, will save it. For what will it profit them to gain the whole world and forfeit their life? Indeed, what can they give in return for their life?'
(Mark 8.34–37)

'Whoever wishes to be first among you must be slave of all. For the Son of Man came not to be served but to serve, and to give his life a ransom for many.'
(Mark 10.44–45)

'You have heard that it was said, "You shall love your neighbour and hate your enemy." But I say to you, Love your enemies and pray for those who persecute you.'
(Matthew 5.43–44)

'No one can serve two masters; for a slave will either hate the one and love the other, or be devoted to the one and despise the other. You cannot serve God and wealth.' (Matthew 6.24)

'Do not worry, saying, "What will we eat?" or "What will we drink?" or "What will we wear?" For it is the Gentiles who strive for all these things; and indeed your heavenly Father knows that you need all these things. But strive first for the kingdom of God and his righteousness, and all these things will be given to you as well. So do not worry about tomorrow, for tomorrow will bring worries of its own. Today's trouble is enough for today.' (Matthew 6.31–34)

'Do not judge, so that you may not be judged. For with the judgement you make you will be judged, and the measure you give will be the measure you get. Why do you see the speck in your neighbour's eye, but do not notice the log in your own eye? Or how can you say to your neighbour, "Let me take the speck out of your eye", while the log is in your own eye? You hypocrite, first take the log out of your own eye, and then you will see clearly to take the speck out of your neighbour's eye.' (Matthew 7.1–5)

'All who exalt themselves will be humbled, and all who humble themselves will be exalted.' (Matthew 23.12)

'Everyone who drinks of this water will be thirsty again, but those who drink of the water that I will give them will never be thirsty. The water that I will give will become in them a spring of water gushing up to eternal life.' (John 4.13–14)

'I came that they may have life, and have it abundantly.' (John 10.10)

Chapters 3, 4 and 5

For reflection and discussion

- What difference does it make to know that Jesus loves you enough to have died for you?
- What does the life of Mary say to you?
- Jesus said he had come to 'bring good news' (Luke 4.18). What might that 'good news' be for you?
- Is there any Gospel story that appeals to you? What might it tell you about Jesus and how you feel about him?

6

The Passion of Christ

The desire to embrace his Father's plan of redeeming love
inspired Jesus' whole life
for his redemptive passion was the very reason for
his Incarnation.
And so he asked, 'And what shall I say?
"Father, save me from this hour"?
No, for this purpose I have come to this hour.'
The Catechism of the Catholic Church, para. 607

಄

Christ Suffered

Seven days before Easter, on what we call Palm Sunday, Jesus rides into Jerusalem on a donkey (Matt. 21) and heralds his Passion, that period in his life when a major shift occurs and he enters most fully into suffering in all its forms.

In his book *The Stature of Waiting*, W. H. Vanstone makes the profound point that, a few days later in the garden of Gethsemane, Jesus – who had always been in control of events – will hand himself into the power of others (Luke 24.7). John's Gospel makes the same point in a different way when, at the Last Supper, Jesus tells Judas to 'Do quickly what you are going to do' (13.27), permitting him to set in motion the train of events leading to his crucifixion.

Here is Jesus – God – placing his life into the hands of his creatures just as he did at his Incarnation except, this time, he knows this will probably mean certain death (John 18.1ff.), for his trial will be a sham, the evidence concocted and the verdict – guilty – already decided. God in Christ clearly joins all those innocent victims of our fear and hatred, blindness and refusal to stand up for justice. He joins in our suffering; is abused, beaten, crowned with thorns and led to crucifixion, something we're able to recall in a powerful way through the devotion known as the *Stations of the Cross*.[1]

This period, from Palm Sunday to Easter Day (Holy Week) culminates in the three most important days of the Christian Year – Maundy Thursday, Good Friday and Holy Saturday. This 'Sacred Triduum' confronts us with ways in which our Faith shows how suffering is intimately connected with life.

What to make of suffering

But if God is good why should there *be* suffering? Couldn't God have created a world where people didn't hurt each other, where Nature was kindly? The Scriptures, especially the psalms, reveal ways in which people have grappled with suffering, even blaming, but always in dialogue with, God (see Ps. 22). The book of Job grapples with this: there you'll find lament, complaint, accusation – but trust that God will not, in the end, abandon Job utterly. We touched on that in Chapter 2, recognizing that suffering is part of the mystery of life and can reveal depths of compassion we might not otherwise experience.

Stations of the Cross are one means of recalling that God in Christ *also* experienced darkness and perplexity, suffering and death, which is also why the crucifix rather than an empty cross is so valuable. For an empty cross might say 'Jesus isn't here', but a cross with the Crucified shows he shares our suffering. When Julian of Norwich (1342–c. 1416) lay in great pain and was close to death she was shown a crucifix by her priest who invited her to look upon it and take strength from this image, leading Julian to a series of profound revelations.[2]

Our forebears, wanting to help us connect our suffering with his, and to show just how *much* Christ suffered, often showed his wounds in graphic detail. You may have seen the famous sixteenth-century Isenheim Altarpiece by Matthias Grünewald which the monks, who cared for victims of plague, placed in their hospital. I remember being deeply moved on kneeling before an ancient statue of the dead Christ and noticing how his body showed the signs of beating, blood pouring from wounds in his head, hands and feet, and knew that all pain and suffering was to be found here.

Those who must stand alongside and behold innocent suffering can also experience its terrors. What must it have been like for Jesus' mother at the foot of the Cross? There she stayed – there love stayed. Would we ever know the depths of love if there were no suffering? For suffering can bring compassion if it unites us with the heart of the Other.

What did *God* experience as Jesus hung there? God-in-Christ must have known immense suffering in order to fully share in this world-changing moment. Apart from the physical, emotional and spiritual suffering, he saw the love of friends and the anguish of his mother – such deep anguish that only a mother can have for her child. He saw the absence of insight in some, the superficiality of others and lack of interest in the onlookers. He saw it all, and more – he saw the depth of his own Heart. Fear was there, yet beneath that and stronger than that, he saw love, love now darkly crowned. And, for one brief moment, he cried in the words of Psalm 22, 'My God, my God, why have you forsaken me?' (Matt. 27.46).

Jesus' death bridged the gap between God and humankind; his obedience – his deep listening – to his Father drew us back together (Rom. 5.19). When I gaze on a crucifix, I see suffering and death, yes, but I also see love blazing from a tree. I see passion and I see *com*passion and I see someone who loves me to the point that they would lay down their life for me. I see what being fully human can mean. What do you see?

Yet I can easily undermine all of this by allowing my attention to be diverted from that sacred, compassionate gaze of God from the Cross and, instead, giving it to a critical glare, blaming myself and refusing to see myself as God does. There have been many times when I've been almost crippled by this critical glare, by a sense of shame at past sins and a refusal to divert my contemplative gaze to the mercy and compassion of God. But if you can't sense that divine gaze, don't be disheartened or discouraged; it can help to talk with a priest or spiritual director – God will be with you, for the heart of God is filled with mercy, pity and compassion for us.

The Sacred Triduum

At the end of Holy Week come three days (the Sacred Triduum) which, since earliest times, Christians have re-enacted in special ways. We can read about them, but what really helps us enter most fully into the events is by becoming part of the drama as it unfolds through powerful, dramatic liturgies when we can share in the scenes.

Maundy Thursday recalls the night which, according to Matthew, Mark and Luke, was Passover when Jews remember their freedom from slavery in Egypt. We do the same whenever the Eucharist is celebrated, for Christianity is all about liberation. On this most holy night Jesus told his disciples, 'abide in my love' (John 15.9) and we remember the depth of that love by washing feet, just as he did.

> *'If you keep my commandments, you will abide in my love, just as I have kept my Father's commandments and abide in his love.'*
> *(John 15.10)*

Then, after the Eucharist of the Last Supper has been celebrated, we process with the Blessed Sacrament (the consecrated bread) to a place where we stay in prayer for an hour. Churches are open until midnight, sometimes throughout the night, to allow people to come and pray. During this time we also dramatically strip the altars recalling how Jesus was stripped of his garments.

Good Friday is a solemn day for all Christians. But it's noticeable that while many are happy to be at church on Easter Day fewer will be present at the liturgy on *this* day. And that's what happened at the crucifixion: when Jesus hung there, only his mother and a few others (including his closest disciple) stayed with him. But if we're to *really* understand our Faith it's important to be with Jesus as he is crucified. And if it's impossible to attend an afternoon service, ask your priest to offer an evening liturgy.

We share in reading the Gospel account of the crucifixion and venerate the Cross, an act which powerfully connects us to the death of Jesus as we are invited to kiss his body. The notion that God (in Christ) suffered and died is repugnant to some and plain stupid to others, but it shows that new life comes at a cost; it doesn't come when you choose as you might decide on a makeover. It comes when we're prepared to let go into the arms of God, requiring a deep sense of trust.

Holy Saturday completes the Triduum and commemorates the time Jesus spent amongst the dead (1 Peter 4.6) and will be considered when we come to that part of the Creed which says that 'he descended to the dead'.

These ancient services, offering a powerful doorway into the mystery of Christ, encompass the heart of Christianity and show how it is the costly antidote to so much superficiality masquerading as offering a better life. Perhaps the motto of the Passion might be, 'I'm dying to live.' Participation in these three days will deepen our faith if we embrace rather than avoid them.

❧

Christ Died

Yet for St John the Divine, Christ's death was a victory; the moment which accomplished all that his life had been about (19.30) – an offering of perfect obedience to the Father for the sake of the world which opens the way to life (1 Cor. 15.22).

> *The Passion of Christ is the greatest and most stupendous work of Divine Love. The greatest and most overwhelming work of God's love.*[3]

Jesus loved to the end and fulfilled the Will of God. That's what I saw when I first gazed on the crucifix when I was 17 – I saw what love looks like. Crucified love blazing with glory; his body given for me, his blood shed for us.

Self-abandonment

One of the hardest things we can do in life is to let go of something precious, and life is the most precious gift we have. What must Jesus have gone through as he realized he would have to give up his? You get a sense of what must have gone on in his heart when he reprimands Peter (Matt. 16.21–23) for trying to persuade him not to jeopardize his life in those chilling words: 'Get behind me, Satan! You are a stumbling-block to me; for you are setting your mind not on divine things but on human things.'

Many who face the choice between life and death will experience similar agonizing feelings. From the martyrs of the early Christian era to those in our own time the question is whether to run and live or face letting go to certain death. We may not have to face that stark choice but, in many ways, we're invited to let go of something – what might that be for you? A prejudice, fear, jealousy? Sense of injustice? Greed? Inability to stop spending on unnecessary things? Harking back to some imaginary rosy past? Constant self-criticism? People pleasing? Inability to let go of shame? The list is endless, but we can start letting go of these right now and it helps if there's something with a stronger appeal urging us to do so. I remember the time when, fearing to swim out of my depth, I began snorkelling among the coral of the Gulf of Aqaba and as its beauty attracted me, so I began to swim into deeper water – and my fear disappeared.

If we have abandoned ourselves to God, there is only one rule for us: the duty of the present moment.[4]

Losing life

The final act of abandonment comes with death. As we look to that moment – especially during the autumn of our days – we can be filled with fear at the prospect of increasing diminishment. That's very understandable – Jesus wept at the tomb of his friend Lazarus and later prayed he would be spared suffering and death:

'My Father, if it is possible, let this cup pass from me.'
(Matthew 26.39)

Facing illness or the gradual loss of our faculties can be frightening. Some will become house-bound or room-bound and need to give away much of what they possess, which might fill us with anxiety or bitterness. Or can we bid farewell to all that has been with a heart thankful for what they've given? And when we revisit the past can we do so with a compassionate, thankful gaze rather than one that causes us to become ossified? All this can be helped by developing a daily practice of 'letting go'.

Death might be 'natural', but it can feel utterly unnatural – this cannot happen! Thoughts about it can be accompanied with sadness, despair and a fear at entering what can seem eternal darkness. Yet:

Even darkness is not darkness to you;
the night shall be as bright as day;
and the darkness the same as light.
(Psalm 139.12)

What cannot be taken from us is our *inner* life, our life with Christ. Rather than giving our attention to the noise and mind-numbing game shows which fill the TV lounges of many residential homes, we need to 'set our minds on Christ' (Col. 3.2f.). It's then that the relationship we have built with God will be of great importance – as might a prayer as simple as letting the beads of a rosary move wordlessly through our fingers. We need to learn to die daily – to sin and self.

But even if we lose touch with life the deep, silent place where the soul resides remains. I vividly recall, when saying Mass at a local dementia home, the way some patients would respond to old hymn tunes, the flicker of a candle or the sight of vestments.

For Jesus, too, the time came when he needed to let go of holding onto *his* life – could you do that? It can be a very lonely movement, as the final journey is one that can only be made in the company of the angels and saints, but it's the journey we can begin now.

Rotten apples

Jesus' death wasn't the fault of any particular group for none are innocent of sin – that religious word concerning everything separating us from God, everything which causes disharmony and death which he overcame.

It began with the apple that tempted Eve and Adam; appealingly glossy on the outside but inside full of rottenness. Pride, greed, lust, envy, gluttony, anger and laziness – the 'seven deadly sins' – affect us all and, although they might not seem deadly, can poison individuals *and* societies. Leaders can seek to seduce us by using nationalism masquerading as patriotism, corporate greed, lust for power, casual racism and so on. Jesus stands with all those who challenge such views and he, like so many, paid the price. Whose side are we on?

The Lamb of God

At his Baptism, John the Baptist had said of Jesus: 'Here is the Lamb of God who takes away the sin of the world!' (John 1.29). A lamb was highly prized and sacrificed at Passover to recall how the Jews had been liberated from slavery (Ex. 12.1ff.) and the crucifixion is understood to involve Jesus' offering his life for the same end. Maybe you remember that, just before receiving Holy Communion (the Body and Blood of Christ), the priest recalls this moment by showing the Blessed Sacrament, saying:

> *Behold the Lamb of God, behold him who takes away the sin of the world.*
> *Blessed are those who are called to the supper of the Lamb.*

Here is our God-made-Man hanging on the Cross. Not an all-mighty, ever-powerful Lord but someone naked and vulnerable. That is the uniqueness of our faith: the God in whom we believe, the maker of heaven and earth, was prepared to know what it is to be human, to be weak, frightened and lonely, just as you and I can be. That's why people have been drawn to and by this moment. It's what's inspired great artists, writers, musicians and poets who identify with Jesus hanging, dying, on the Cross.

Some are drawn by the apparent nonsense of it all. They look at the vulnerability of Divine Love and see in sweating, bruised, torn flesh, in fear and loneliness, vulnerability and passion, a glimpse of themselves. Can you identify with God in his broken humanity? Can you see your wounds reflected in his? Wounds which, as someone once wrote to me, are to be found everywhere: 'To kiss the wounds of Jesus, to enter into the wounds of Jesus, just go out into the street.'

It was at this moment Jesus fulfilled – accomplished – the purpose of his life. Not to appease an angry god but to be faithful to his Father who lived in perfect union with him. Jesus chose to see this through to the bitter end and his Father would not save him from his calling. As he had said to his disciples: 'No one has greater love than this, to lay down one's life for one's friends. You are my friends if you do what I command you' (John 15.14).

Redemption and salvation

At the heart of all this lie these two religious words: 'redemption', meaning to 'buy back', and 'salvation', meaning to be saved. Both concern the way people have experienced needing to be freed from sin – from the grip of deathly forces – and have found in Jesus the person who can bring them to the light of life.

Even when people are losing interest in religion this need for a saviour remains strong. Sadly, many are more attracted by the person who claims they will make everything right: strong-willed political or religious 'charismatic' leaders who usually turn out to be demagogues and dictators. For others 'being saved' from a variety of addictions is a matter of life and death and they know that only a 'Power' greater than themselves can do that, which is when they decide to hand themselves over to God's care.[5]

Arguably those who deny they're enthralled by anything,

that they're completely free, are deluding themselves, for at best we're on the road to liberation – being saved, redeemed, for that wholeness of life for which we were created.

> *O Saviour of the world,*
> *who by Thy Cross and precious Blood hast redeemed us:*
> *save us, and help us,*
> *we humbly beseech Thee, O Lord.*[6]

What is of greatest help on this way is to know that we are held in the compassionate heart of the One who loves us and, seeing our brokenness, longs for our wholeness. We need a redeemer in whom we can trust, whose heart will embrace us and never let us go – and the central mystery of our Faith is that through the way of suffering and death comes life.

Atonement

This brings us to one of the most important themes in Christianity – reconciliation or, to use a religious word, atonement, something you find talked about throughout the New Testament. 'For if while we were enemies, we were reconciled to God through the death of his Son, much more surely, having been reconciled, will we be saved by his life' (Rom. 5.10). The early Christians saw Jesus as the One who fulfilled the Law and to 'live in him' was to be free of those demands, provided one lived by the 'law of love' (Rom. 13.8–10). Maybe that's why so many liberation movements have sprung up in Christian cultures, from the liberation of slaves, to gays and lesbians. Humanity was created to be free and as we are made one with Christ, so we say 'yes' to his gift of freedom.

Some believe that Christ's death 'satisfied' the 'wrath' of God against sin. But doesn't that paint God as some monstrous father whose anger can only be satisfied by the death of his son? That's not what Jesus, the enfleshment of God, revealed about the divine nature through his life and teachings. Far more importantly, his death reveals that love overcomes all – even anger.

> For I saw no wrath in God ... except on man's side, and he forgives that in us, for wrath is nothing but a perversity and an opposition to peace and to love.[7]

࿇

Christ descended to the dead

On Good Friday the Liturgy of the Day ends in silence as people leave the church and many think what follows, Holy Saturday, is a 'day of rest' or one of 'waiting and watching'. But why neglect his burial? St Ephrem the Syrian (c. 306–373) knew better and beautifully captures the significance of this day in an Easter sermon:

> When by a loud cry from that cross Jesus summoned the dead from the underworld, death was powerless to prevent it ... his godhead engaged death in combat ... It was able to kill natural human life, but was itself killed by the life that is above the nature of man ... He came in search of a chariot in which to ride to the underworld. This chariot was the body which he received from the Virgin; in it he invaded death's fortress, broke open its strong room and scattered all its treasure.

This theology/spirituality of the 'harrowing of hell', when Christ descended to the realm of the dead to liberate us, emerges from various scriptural references (e.g. 1 Peter 3.18b–19 and 4.6). There's something of deep significance in

Christ's journey into the realm of Death, for the effect of his redemption works at both a conscious and unconscious level, affecting the whole cosmic order. Carl Jung said it also represents the ego's deliberate descent into the unconscious where it emerges reborn.[8]

This great event, celebrated in the (neglected) Liturgy of the Burial of Christ (see Appendix 4), is portrayed in orthodox icons by the image of his descent into that darkness. He breaks into the prison-house of death and drags Adam and Eve, our archetypal ancestors, from sleep into the light of his Divinity. This, arguably, is the great moment of salvation – his victory which redeems all humankind, even back to the beginning. And our ceaseless task is to open ourselves more and more deeply to Christ's gracious, compassionate invitation to be set free.

When in the new tomb you,
the Redeemer of all, had been laid for the sake of all,
hell became a laughing stock and, seeing you, quaked
*   with fear;*
the bars were smashed, the gates were shattered,
the graves were opened, the dead arose ...
When you went down to death, O immortal Life,
you slew hell with the lightning flash of your Godhead.[9]

∾

Invitation:

Find a crucifix and spend some time gazing on the figure of Jesus. What do you notice? Is there anything you want to say to him?

Notes

1 *Stations of the Cross* is a devotion concerning 14 moments on the journey Jesus made from his trial before Pilate to his Entombment. With hymns and prayers those 'making the Stations' walk with Christ and stop to re-member – literally. The devotion began during the Middle Ages when it was difficult for Christians to visit Jerusalem and so churches installed plaques on their walls to enable people to connect with the events depicted and to realize something of Jesus' suffering.

2 Julian of Norwich, *Revelations of Divine Love*, Oxford University Press, 2015, ch. 3.

3 St Paul of the Cross (1694–1775), *Letters*, L. 11, 499.

4 Jean-Pierre de Caussade SJ (1675–1751), *Abandonment to Divine Providence*, The Catholic Records Press, Book 2, ch. 2, p. 57.

5 See the '12 Steps of Alcoholics Anonymous'.

6 Order for the Visitation of the Sick, Sarum Manual, and 1549, 1552, 1662 Prayer Books.

7 *Revelations of Divine Love*, chapters 13 and 58.

8 E. F. Edinger, *The Christian Archetype*, Inner City Books, 1987, p. 110, and C. G. Jung, *Aion*, Routledge, 1991, CW9ii, para. 72.

9 The Good Friday Matins of Great Saturday.

7

Rising, You Restored Our Life

Now all things have been filled with light,
both heaven and earth and those beneath the earth;
so let all creation sing Christ's rising,
by which it is established.
St John of Damascus (c. 675–749)

❧

The first time I travelled through Maundy Thursday to Holy Saturday was a revelation, for I discovered the treasures these days reveal. Just as there's a difference between reading a play and taking part in it, I suddenly found myself entering the mysteries of Christ's Passion. If you've travelled through them you'll probably understand why we do what Christians have done since the very earliest times – re-enact the story.

At the great Vigil liturgy on Easter Day (or on the night of Holy Saturday) people carry into dim churches – symbolizing the tomb of Jesus – the great Paschal Candle, the Light of Christ, proclaiming that darkness has been overcome. From it, people light their own candle affirming they want to share in resurrection life.

There *is* a struggle going on – a cosmic struggle – and the forces of darkness, suffering and death often find it easy to win the day. But they cannot, in the end, win the battle for that was won by Jesus as he faced down the forces of evil. Of course, all this is scandalous to many; ever since the dawn of Christianity people have argued that Jesus could never have risen from the dead: that it's all a myth, an invention of the disciples; that Jesus only fainted on the cross; that God would never let someone as important as him die a scoun-drel's death. And, no doubt, the arguments will go on. For Christianity is a faith, not a science. St Paul, in his First Letter to the Church in Corinth, says:

> *If for this life only we have hoped in Christ, we are of all people most to be pitied.*
> *(15.19)*

He wants us to see this event in cosmic dimensions because Christ's resurrection is for this world and the whole creation, for now and eternity, and it all hinges on the briefest of encounters. A triumph known in the stillness of a garden at dawn (John 20.11ff.); at evening when bread was broken (Luke 24.30ff.); in an upper room whose doors were locked for fear (John 20.19ff.); by a lake as day broke (John 21.1ff.). Fleeting encounters with women and men who had no cause to hope in more than what humdrum everyday life offered in this outpost of the Roman Empire.

How could these fishermen and housewives, workers and prostitutes be so sure that something so stupendous had happened? They couldn't. What they noticed, what they began to wonder about, was that life had changed. Their eyes were being opened to something quite new. Christianity didn't first spread through force of arms but because ordinary men and women discovered that Christ had risen from the dead. Would those who knew him give their lives, as many did, if they weren't convinced that Jesus had overcome death and opened the way to life eternal?

Yet even if someone 'proved' Jesus physically rose from the dead, what difference would it make? Instead, take the resurrection to heart and ponder its consequence. Like Mary Magdalene, try looking through the misty dawn and listen for the voice of Jesus calling you, as he called her (John 20.16ff.). 'Mary,' he said, and she slowly discovered who it was that spoke her name. God is always calling us into his new life, which can be accessed in our hearts as we 'put to death' our old nature (Rom. 6.6) and become bearers of the truth that sin and death are not the end – for Life has triumphed.

Awake sleeper, I have not made you to be held a prisoner in the underworld.
Arise from the dead; I am the life of the dead.
Arise, you that are the work of my hands, arise you that were fashioned in my image.
Rise, let us go hence; for you in me and I in you, together we are one undivided person.[1]

Invitation:

Sit quietly before a lighted candle. See its brightness and imagine its beam piercing into the darkness within you. Is there any place in your heart that is closed off, locked and bolted? A place you're afraid to enter? Spend some minutes letting the brightness of that candle beam gently melt your heart and allow Christ to set you free.

Note

1 From an ancient homily for Holy Saturday.

8

Humanity Taken into Heaven

In the first creation He gave me myself;
but in His new creation He gave me Himself,
and by that gift restored to me the self that I had lost.
Created first and then restored,
I owe Him myself twice over in return for myself.
St Bernard of Clairvaux (1090–1153)

❧

When I was a child, you could take a half-morning off from school on Ascension Day to attend a service celebrating Christ's passing into heaven (Luke 24.50–51 and Acts 1.6–11). Now this event seems forgotten, which is a real loss; for not only does it affirm the Ascension of Christ but also that our complete humanity has been taken into God. As St Irenaeus said in the second century:

The Word of God was made that which we are, in order that He might perfect us to be what He is.[1]

That's one of the most beautiful statements of our Faith: we're invited to realize our divinity. Just as the whole of creation was embraced by God in the Incarnation so that same Creation is now taken into Divinity by the Ascension of Christ. It invites us to consider to what we give attention – on what or whom our heart is set. Isn't it easy to be caught up in the humdrum matters of life, to allow our – often difficult or painful – experiences to imprison us? So, when I find myself glued to my own inner iPod, listening to the same old 'tunes' over and over again, I try to remember that I need to be released from them that I might become what God is making me to be. To be present to Christ just as he, in his glory, is present to me. That's what the Ascension is all about.

Some people think that faith is about escaping the 'flesh' – it's only the spiritual that matters. Yet flesh and spirit, mind and body, are one: the Ascension fulfils the Incarnation, for when Christ entered heaven it was with the marks of the crucifixion still on his body.

The whole of us is to be taken into glory and this is God's way of saying 'You belong with me. Because I created you, you are precious in my sight. Whatever you have done I love you and want you with me where I am. You are of such worth to me that I died for you and now enfold you into my Heart.'

Our worth isn't dependent on anything we've done but is simply consequent on our being God's creation: flawed and broken, yes, but with endless value to our Creator.

&

Draw me, Lord,
into the fullness of Life;
cleanse me
from all that separates me from you;

open my eyes
to the glory set before me,
and never let me be parted from you.
Amen.

❧

Invitation:

Sit quietly, breathe deeply and imagine being enfolded in God's Heart. How does that feel and how might you respond?

Note

1 John Keble, *Library of Fathers of the Holy Catholic Church*, Sagwan Press, 2018, p. 449.

9

Judged by Our Loving

And now, O Master, let Thy hand shelter me,
and let Thy mercy come upon me.
St Eustratius (fourth century)

Success and failure

So often we judge ourselves and others by material success
– having the latest, most expensive car, glamorous holidays,
brilliant career – and can be awestruck by the apparently
gilded lives of celebrities. But none of that counts with God.

In the eyes of the world Jesus' life was a failure – even most
of his disciples left him when he was arrested and crucified.
But in God's sight it was his faithfulness that mattered; God
doesn't judge us by the clothes we wear or the people we know,
but by the way we've sought to live with love. Ultimately
there'll come a final judgement, something we look forward
to each Advent, but only God knows when this will be.

God's judgement

So if you worry about being judged and found wanting – 'How
do people react to me: do they like me, find me interesting?
Am I getting it right?' – consider how your heart is set. God
asks that we try to live lovingly but realizes we won't always
get it right. Unfortunately, there are those who reject people
because of who and what they are, but that's wrong, for such
views don't reflect a compassionate God.

Jesus was quite clear about God's judgement and told some very powerful stories to illustrate his teaching (Matt. 25.31–46). Take a look at them and notice that they concern how we've cared for others, which led St John of the Cross to declare that: 'At the end of our days we will be judged by our loving.'[1] It's Love by which we'll be judged, Love whose mercy is never ending (see Lam. 3.22ff.).

Give rest, O Christ,
to thy servant with thy saints,
where sorrow and pain are no more;
neither sighing, but life everlasting.
Thou only art immortal,
the Creator and Maker of man;
and we are mortal, formed of the earth,
and unto earth shall we return;
for so thou didst ordain
when thou createdst me, saying:
'Dust thou art, and unto dust shalt thou return.'
All we go down to the dust,
and, weeping o'er the grave we make our song:
Alleluia, alleluia, alleluia.[2]

࿊

Invitation:

Write your own obituary. Ask God to reveal to you the truth about your life beneath what you may feel. When were you most open to responding to love? When did you fail to act with generosity towards others – towards yourself? Or fail to trust God? What would you want to celebrate?

Notes

1 John of the Cross, *Sayings of Light and Love*, Westminster Roman Catholic Diocesan Trust, 2011.

2 *Contakion for the Dead*, hymn from the Orthodox service for the repose of the departed.

Chapters 5, 6, 7, 8 and 9

For reflection and discussion

- Read the passages referred to in 5a. What stands out? What does that say to you about Christian living?
- In what way might Jesus' Passion and Death speak into our experience of suffering?
- What makes it difficult to let go of things?
- In what ways are the seven 'Deadly Sins' deadly?
- What are the problems associated with looking for a 'saviour'?
- Read John 21.1–18. Imagine yourself in the garden with Peter, John and Mary Magdalene. What do you notice about the way each of them responds? What do you wonder about the way they encountered the empty tomb? How do these affect your perception of the Resurrection?
- Where might you find 'new life'? How does this affect the way you live?
- What might God say to you when you come to stand before him? What might you want to say to God?

SANCTIFIER

Breathe in me, O Holy Spirit,
that my thoughts may all be holy.
Act in me, O Holy Spirit, that my work, too, may be holy.
Draw my heart, O Holy Spirit, that I love but what is holy.
Strengthen me, O Holy Spirit, to defend all that is holy.
Guard me, then, O Holy Spirit, that I always may be holy.
Amen.
St Augustine of Hippo

The Go-Between God

Enrich your soul in the great goodness of God:
The Father is your table, the Son is your food,
and the Holy Spirit waits on you
and then makes His dwelling in you.
St Catherine of Siena

჻

When you hear of the 'Holy Spirit' I wonder what's conjured up in your mind? There are lots of people who've never heard of this third Person of the Trinity whom one writer referred to as the 'go-between' God,[1] the One constantly moving from Father through Son in an outpouring of love.

I'd often prayed for the guidance of the Spirit, but when I lived at Alnmouth friary in 1978 I met a group of Sisters who 'prayed in the Spirit'. They were so enthusiastic that I decided I wanted what they had and earnestly asked God for the same experience and that my faith would glow like theirs. That wasn't to be, at least not in the way I'd wanted. Instead as I was praying one day, I heard a voice saying: 'What is that to you? Follow me!' And from then on, I stopped worrying and decided to trust God.

჻

Creative Spirit

The fact is the Spirit fills all things – is never absent from us – but we can be blind to her presence. As I write this, I've just returned from walking on the nearby hilly slopes overlooking the Thames basin: the wind flowed around me and, after a long period of drought, grass is beginning to grow again as it soaks up the recent rain. I smelled the dampness of soil and was filled with a deep sense of life and recalled the second verse of the Bible:

> ... *the earth was a formless void and darkness covered the face of the deep,*
> *while a wind from God swept over the face of the waters.*

The Spirit has always been understood as that wind, the 'breath' of God, which swept over the primeval chaos showing that, before anything else, God is intimately connected to the earth.

> *By the breath of God ice is given,*
> *and the broad waters are frozen fast.*
> *He loads the thick cloud with moisture;*
> *the clouds scatter his lightning.*
> *(Job 37.10–11)*

I love this elemental aspect of the Holy Spirit: when I'm buffeted by winds or gently caressed by breezes I'm being permeated by God in a fundamental way. Later the Spirit will bring back to life that which is dead when Ezekiel is told that the breath of God will come with the four winds to revive those slain in battle (Ezek. 37.9).

> *Breathe on me, Breath of God,*
> *fill me with life anew.*[2]

☙

Revealing Spirit

The Holy Spirit is also understood as the One who reveals, not least through prophets (Isa. 61.1). Unlike Satan who confuses and obscures, the Spirit enlightens and discloses new things (Isa. 43.19). And the greatest thing the Spirit will do is to reveal the One God will send to bring about a new creation – the Messiah, the 'Anointed One':

> *A shoot shall come out from the stock of Jesse,*
> *and a branch shall grow out of his roots.*
> *The spirit of the Lord shall rest on him,*
> *the spirit of wisdom and understanding,*
> *the spirit of counsel and might,*
> *the spirit of knowledge and the fear of the Lord.*
> *(Isaiah 11.1–3)*

Apart from individual prophets such as Isaiah and Jeremiah there were also communities of prophets, filled with the Spirit (1 Sam. 10.5) who lived in the wilderness and Religious Life looks back to this tradition – of people being drawn by the Holy Spirit into the desert – as one of its roots. What I have grown to know about this revealing nature of the Spirit is the way it searches the hidden depths of God (1 Cor. 2.10) and of *me* for my own good. So, the Spirit has been associated with Holy Wisdom (Wis. 7.22ff.) who longs for me to know the wonder of God and my own being. Opening ourselves to the work of the Spirit will involve discovering more of the beauty, complexity and hiddenness of who I am, for the key to knowing God has always been to 'know thyself'. Growth in faith is to be accompanied by this growth in self-awareness and acceptance.

ॐ

Liberating Spirit

'The Spirit frees hearts chained by fear,' said Pope Francis on the Feast of Pentecost 2018. There are many who need that freedom, many who are pressured to appear self-reliant or don't feel 'good enough', who need to present themselves as better than others, self-confident, and so on. But there can be a loneliness in their heart and some, rather than nurturing their souls, try to cope through abusive addictions or self-harming.

Right at the start of Jesus' ministry (Luke 4.16ff.) he quoted the prophet Isaiah saying that the Spirit had anointed him to:

- bring good news to the poor;
- proclaim release to captives;
- give sight to the blind;
- set the oppressed free.

Whatever else the Spirit does, it seeks to set us free, which can be very painful and threatening. I wonder if there's anything you need to ask to be freed from? What sort of relationship with God would help? These are questions you could talk through with a spiritual director.

❦

Life-giving Spirit

St Luke tells us that 50 days after Easter, on the Jewish Feast of Pentecost, an event occurred which had a profound effect on the future of humanity. The disciples, including Mary, had gathered in the same Upper Room where they'd met with Jesus for their final Passover celebration, when the Holy Spirit in the form of wind suddenly swept over them and 'tongues of fire' descended (Acts 2). This is the moment when the Church was born, and the apostles went on to preach the gospel throughout the known world.

Some Pentecostal/charismatic churches focus on this exuberant activity of the Spirit. People might speak in strange languages – a sign, they believe, of God's presence because the gift of the Spirit at Pentecost made it possible for the apostles to be heard speaking in 'native languages' (Acts 2.5ff.). St Paul knew all about this but reminded Christians that:

> *If I speak in the tongues of mortals and of angels, but do*
> *   not have love,*
> *I am a noisy gong or a clanging cymbal.*
> *(1 Corinthians 13.1)*

❧

Gifts of the Spirit

Paul would have known that Isaiah said (Isa. 11.2f.) there were six gifts the Spirit gives: wisdom, understanding, counsel, strength, knowledge and piety, but went on to say that each of us also shares in various other gifts because they're for the good of the Body of Christ (1 Cor. 12.1–11). He also talked about the way the Spirit produces 'fruits' in us which he lists as: love, joy, peace, patience, kindness, goodness, faithfulness, gentleness and self-control (Gal. 5.22–23). But the most important gift the Spirit gives is love (1 Cor. 13) which trumps all the others and is the outpouring of the go-between God:

> *For now we see in a mirror, dimly, but then we will see*
> *face to face. Now I know only in part; then I will know*
> *fully, even as I have been fully known. And now faith,*
> *hope, and love abide, these three; and the greatest of*
> *these is love.*
> *(13.12–13)*

❧

Our spirit

These days there's a lot of attention being given to the importance of exercise – gyms are springing up everywhere and
various forms of marathon seem to happen most weekends.

Thankfully, some realize that it's also important to undertake spiritual exercises, something earlier generations and
other cultures have taken for granted. We might spend a
fortune on our bodies, but what attention do we give to our
inner world? Our soul – that part of our being breathed into
us by God? Sadly, when the 'spiritual' *is* addressed it's often
in various esoteric forms that have little to do with the rest of
life. Going 'into retreat' can be about getting away from it all,
yet I recall that one of the most powerful retreats I undertook
was at a flat on a deprived estate in a large city.

We're spiritual as well as material beings in whom God's
image dwells. This is what allows our participation in Divine
life and love and enables grace (the help God gives to share
in divine life) to flow. Too many of us are like someone
who owns a very expensive car, keeps it polished, repaints
it from time to time and repairs any damage – but never
looks beneath the bonnet. I remember when, on first visiting
the Holy Land, I encountered people who looked down on
Westerners, believing that as wealthy as they might be they
were poor because they didn't bother with God and ignored
their soul. Those with whom I spoke often said it was their
relationship with God which made them different from brute
beasts, for having a *soul*, a share in the Spirit of God, makes
us human. As we begin to recognize and work with the soul
we not only discover the riches that lie within, but also the
fact that it's from the heart-space which enfolds the soul that
the dynamics of life emerge. Love and hate, jealousy and
generosity, fear, anger, compassion and all the rest.

Christians have long recognized the importance of the heart/
soul and in the tenth century St Simeon the New Theologian

wrote extensively about this. One of his famous dictums was that the mind should descend into the heart and guard it in the time of prayer or, as I first heard this teaching:

Place your mind in your heart and stand in the presence of God all the day.

It's in your heart you find the place where your soul can encounter God and where you are known by God. It's the place where you can be 'naked' with the One who loves and accepts you and where your true identity emerges; where, instead of saying 'I think, therefore I am', you can be open to the fact that: 'I am *known*; therefore I am'. Once we begin to give our lives to God, to say 'thy will be done' or 'Jesus, I trust in you', then a new phase of our life can begin as we recognize that Christ is the Divine 'yeast' which enables the growth into the beauty, wonder and glory of God that was given us in our first creation.

The soul is the spark of the Divine within us where God's breath resides. As we give attention to our soul and explore how it flourishes in union with God, so we can grow in that relationship, for we were created to love God; there's a duet the soul needs to sing with the Spirit and when it does the music floods our heart and we realize the wonder of our being. When, during a visit to her cousin Elizabeth, the pregnant Mary sings her *Magnificat* – 'My soul *magnifies* the Lord' (Luke 1.46–55) – she's saying: as the seed of God germinates in me so my soul, the essence of who I am flourishes. It's a reminder, too, that if thanksgiving underpins what we do then our lives will be enriched.

❧

Being fully human

Many years ago I found myself asking the question posed
at the beginning of this book – 'What's it all about?' It's a
question that's echoed throughout my life, one which was
addressed early on when I joined the Franciscans in 1976
– 'Why have you come?' It's also a question Jesus posed in
different ways. To fishermen he said, 'What do you seek?'
and to some women, 'Who are you looking for?' Maybe it's
the kind of question you find rolling around in your head at
odd moments when you've nothing else to think about: why
am I here? St Ignatius Loyola gives his own answer in the
opening of his *Spiritual Exercises*:

> *The human person is created to praise, reverence and*
> *serve our Lord God, and by this means to save their soul.*

Living in a society that often seems to equate fullness of life
with how much we are able to achieve, it's worth remember-
ing that, for Christians, being fully human is about reflecting
the glory of God. Our high streets may be full of 'Beauty'
shops but what they focus on is only skin-deep. Perhaps our
churches might advertise themselves as places where you
could beautify your soul, a beauty that comes from letting
the Spirit of God flourish within us, letting ourselves flow
with Christ.

&

Come, Holy Spirit,
and heal my soul.
With you all is possible;
you gave me life –
now I turn my heart to you.
Renew your presence in me
and, through your Wisdom,
may I come to the light of life
that my soul may sing to you
as I reach out to serve your creation.
Amen.

❧

Invitation:

What gifts and fruits of the Spirit are you gifted with – and
are there any you need to pray for?

Notes

1 John V. Taylor, *The Go-Between God*, SCM Classics, 2010.
2 Edwin Hatch (1835–1889).

Chapter 10

For reflection and discussion

- In what ways might the Holy Spirit appeal to you?
- What does the 'Holy Spirit' mean for you? In what ways might you experience the Spirit of God?
- Read 1 Corinthians 13 slowly, replacing 'I' with your name. What do you notice?

11

The Soul's Desire

To pray and love, that is the happiness of man on earth.
St Jean-Marie Vianney (1786–1859)

❧

Many years ago, when I was on pilgrimage in Jerusalem, I became caught up in an incident in the Old City and was rescued by a young Muslim who took me into his home. He apologized for the fact that while his mother would serve us coffee she wouldn't talk for, since the death of her husband, she had taken a vow of constant prayer. And there, on her prayer mat, she knelt.

> *Rejoice always, pray without ceasing, give thanks in all circumstances; for this is the will of God in Christ Jesus for you.*
> *(1 Thessalonians 5.16–18)*

In considering the activity of the Holy Spirit, we need to remember that it's not we who pray but the Spirit who prays within us (Rom. 8.26f.). But if that's so, *why* pray?

I'd like to suggest that prayer is not only a natural activity we turn to, especially at certain times, but that it opens us to the mysteries of God. Mindfulness, rooted in ancient practices of Christian meditation, has awoken many to the importance of attending to the inner life, but prayer takes us further. It enables us to be open to God and so become more fully human. Prayer is about creating a space for God:

*Likewise, the Spirit helps us in our weakness; for we do
not know how to pray as we ought, but that very Spirit
intercedes with sighs too deep for words. And God, who
searches the heart, knows what is the mind of the Spirit,
because the Spirit intercedes for the saints according to
the will of God.*
(Romans 8.26–28)

Prayer is the response of the heart to Love expressed by praise
and thanksgiving, penitence and intercession and deepened
by meditation and contemplation.

> *Prayer is not a thing you do*
> *but something you can become*
> *when the heart is fixed on God.*

❧

A Hidden Treasure

When Jesus was asked how his disciples should pray (Luke
11.1) he told them to say:

> *Father, hallowed be your name.*
>   *Your kingdom come.*
> *Give us each day our daily bread.*
>   *And forgive us our sins,*
>   *for we ourselves forgive everyone indebted to us.*
> *And do not bring us to the time of trial.*

And I imagine one of them replying: 'What – is that it? Is that
what you do all night?' And he might have replied, 'Yes',
because those brief words open a vast treasury of prayer.
I've known people say they can't move beyond saying 'Our

Father' because those two words draw them into that loving relationship.

Prayer opens the heart to God and it's important that we give it time and attention. Some are taught it involves ACTS – *Adoration, Confession, Thanksgiving, Supplication* and each of those aspects can be present when we pray. But I want to suggest that, at heart, prayer is about a love affair with God: you encounter God and, gradually, find you are drawn more and more deeply into a relationship until Love fills your heart:

> *Prayer is an aspiration of the heart. It is a simple glance directed to Heaven. It is a cry of gratitude and love in the midst of trial as well as joy ... it is something great, supernatural, which expands my soul and unites me to Jesus.*[1]

A cry of gratitude

That 'cry of gratitude' reminds me that, just as lovers are deeply thankful for each other, so part of the secret to living prayerfully involves the development of a thankful heart. Each day the official Prayer of the Church begins with a simple yet profound plea: 'O Lord, open our lips', to which we reply: 'And our mouth shall proclaim your praise', before going on to pray Psalm 95:

> *Come, let us sing out our joy to the Lord;*
> *hail the rock who saves us.*

This joyful song of praise sets the tone for the day. I can be a bit grumpy in the morning and sometimes forget to say 'thank you', but a thankful heart is not only a joyful one but also one that can discover that peace which is beyond our understanding. And remember that the heart of the Church's worship is thanksgiving – *eucharist*: thanksgiving changes things.

Intercession

Asking for something on behalf of another might be a natural response to a deeply felt need – 'Oh God, let Mary get better!' But if we're going to ask someone for something, it's best to be in a relationship with them. And when we bring our desires (supplications) to God, we need to trust that God will respond to them in the right way. Our heart might be over-flowing with concerns, but we need to let go of them to God otherwise they can become overwhelming:

Thy will be done
on earth as it is in heaven.

Intercession isn't about getting God to do what we want (no matter how good our intentions); it's learning to open our hearts to God's compassionate love, offering our concerns to Christ (because it's he who prays for us) and then trusting him.

We can offer 'arrow' prayers on the spur of the moment when we're aware of a need or want to give thanks and we can also ask the prayers of the saints – those closest to Jesus. It's like asking our friends to pray for something important, only these are our friends in heaven.

In a room at the Abbey of the Precious Blood in Burnham, there's an icon of 'Our Lady of Intercession' showing Mary holding an open scroll and pointing to words from the account of the wedding feast at Cana: 'They have no wine' (John 2.3). As Sr Margaret Mary SPB wrote:

(Mary) just connects Jesus with the disaster through her own concern. In intercession we, the intercessors, need

to know something of the circumstances to kindle our
concern. God already knows it all, but it seems in the
mystery of humanity where God has given us free will, he
will not bypass this and treat us as robots. Our love and
concern seem to open the way for God's energy to flow
into the world.[2]

&

The Body in Prayer

Our first experience of prayer can often be through worship
as we step out of our everyday world and enter the mystery of
God's presence. And because we're made up of soul *and* body
what we do with the latter in worship can be of great help,
so let's look at various ways in which what we do physically
can aid our prayer.

Sign of the Cross

Many find making the Sign of the Cross, accompanied with
the words, 'In the name of the Father, + and of the Son and
of the Holy Spirit' to be very helpful. Touching first the fore-
head, then the breast, left and right shoulder connects us with
the heart of our Faith.

I remember feeling embarrassed when I first did this in
church, but knew I wanted to express something powerful,
to connect myself with the Crucified, and wasn't going to let
my fear of what others *might* think stop me. Many churches
allow us to reaffirm our baptism by providing a 'stoup' (a con-
tainer) of water blessed by a priest at the entrance into which
we can dip our fingers and make the Sign as we enter or leave.
Some do so on beginning a journey, before going to sleep
or on waking, at the news of a death or as a funeral passes.

Whatever the circumstance it's a reminder and acceptance of all that our Faith teaches about the love of God manifested in the Passion of Christ.

Standing

This is the most ancient way to pray as it shows respect and readiness to act. It's associated with paying attention, which is why we stand when the Gospel's read and the Eucharistic Prayer offered, and was the position in which early Christians interceded and prayed to the Our Father who has raised us up. When the Faith spread into cultures where kneeling was the position of servitude, standing straight, tall and free had special meaning for early believers, something we still recall in one of the Eucharistic Prayers:

> ... we thank you for counting us worthy to stand in your presence and serve you.

Of course, people have always sat if necessary, but standing affirms that we're not onlookers, but participants.

Kneeling

Kneeling is a sign of penance, supplication and adoration and after the Reformation became a sign of human unworthiness.

Genuflecting

This profound sign of respect, when you briefly bend one knee to the ground whenever passing the Sacrament, is like showing respect to the monarch when you are in their presence. A white light burns in places where the Blessed Sacrament is reserved.

Bowing

It's a popular tradition to bow slightly when the name of Jesus (and, sometimes, Mary) is mentioned in the liturgy, or during the *Gloria* (Glory be to the Father ...) or deeply when passing an altar, which symbolises the sacrificial body of Christ.

Hands

Hands work hard for us but can be neglected as a means of prayer. From using them to make the Sign of the Cross to raising them in prayer, they help affirm our faith. Some Christians practise praying with hands raised in a gesture of receiving or giving. This can be a powerful communal act and has remained the prayer position of priests when celebrating the Eucharist.

The Rosary

Fingers help focus our attention when praying the Rosary.[3] This is a means of praying with the 'Mysteries' of the life of Christ and Mary involving mostly Gospel events known as 'Joyful', 'Luminous', 'Sorrowful' and 'Glorious'. Another form of rosary is used to assist praying the Jesus Prayer, as you allow your fingers to move over knotted beads. Most religions realize the value of having something to hold in the fingers to help deal with distractions.

Incense

Offered to Jesus at his birth, incense has been used in worship since ancient times. The rising smoke engages our senses and symbolizes that God is hidden from sight:

Let my prayer be accepted as incense before you,
the raising of my hands like an evening oblation.
(Psalm 141.2)

The book of Revelation tells us that, in heaven, incense – symbolizing the 'prayers of God's people' – is constantly offered to God (8.4) and it was one of the gifts offered by the Magi to the Christchild. Five things are censed at Mass: the altar because it symbolizes Christ; the Book of the Gospels because it contains the word of Christ; the people because they are the body of Christ; the priest who is the icon of Christ; and the Sacrament where Christ is present.

Fasting

If you are waking up to the effects of excessive consumption and the need to develop a deeper awareness of our relationship with the planet you might consider the value of fasting. This can be from food, or the Internet. It's another reminder of the way the body can aid our relationship with God, for fasting both cleanses and sharpens our desire for Divine nourishment. This is why fasting for an hour before receiving the Sacrament is recommended.

Colour

Colour is used to indicate the seasons or particular celebrations when vestments and altar coverings help the senses to aid our devotion. The splendour of gold for the great festivals; white for virginity, birth and those who give their lives without spilling their blood; red for the martyrs and seasons of the Spirit; purple for sorrow and the fasts of Advent and Lent. Black is sometimes used to remind us of the deep sadness of death; rose pink for two Sundays in Advent and Lent when we 'take a breather', and green for everything else in Ordinary Time, reminding us of the way life can flourish in such periods.

Worship is assisted through these sensory ways, and ritual has the power to release emotions enabling us to connect our individual experiences with the personal, communal and universal experiences of humankind. Its loss robs us of timeless ways of connecting with the Divine.

಄

Everyday Contemplation and Mindfulness

Finding time for prayer can seem impossible, but we can all develop methods of 'everyday contemplation', aspects of which form the basis of what has become known as 'Mindfulness'. They're not the same, but the practice of the latter can lead into contemplation. We in the West have forgotten the need to attend to our inner life, but this – thankfully – is changing. One of my parishioners told me how she practised meditation with her children for ten minutes before supper each day, and many schools are adding it to their curriculum to help children learn how to keep focused, deal with unwanted distractions, develop an inner calmness and stop worrying.

Many of us don't meditate, or think it's only for monks and nuns, yet meditation and contemplation, the deepest forms of prayer, are for all. It's usually possible to find time when you can simply stop for a while and turn your heart to God – on the train coming home from work, at times when you set an alert on your phone or as a clock strikes – to halt the busyness of life. Here are some suggestions to help you develop your own practice:

Slow down. Walk more slowly, cycle more gently (the journey's also important) and breathe more deeply.

Stop and be, even for a minute.

Pay attention. Give your whole attention to whatever is happening in this moment – the person you're with, the painting you're looking at or the view out of the bus window.

A long, loving look at the real. Go into a garden or park and take a long, deep, loving look at everything you see.

Engaging your senses. When you walk down the street notice everything around you by utilizing all your senses and give thanks for the presence of God in all things.

And if you find that your mind is overactive – full of noisy parakeets flying all over the place – train yourself not to give them your attention. The more you do so the worse they become.

Heart prayer

'Prayer of the Heart' engages the rhythm of our breathing to help us deepen prayer and can be practised whenever and wherever you are. Simply 'watching' our breath as it descends into the heart connects us with the Spirit who animates all things and is an intimate form of prayer.

Dom John Main, an English Benedictine, developed a mantra (rhythmic prayer) recommended by the World Community for Christian Meditation (WCCM), in which a single word is used – *Maranatha* (Come, Lord) for example. Again, using the breath one silently prays:

Ma-ra
inhaling and
na-tha
exhaling.

In the nineteenth century a Russian pilgrim, seeking to grow in prayer, was initiated into another form of rhythmic prayer, now known as the Jesus Prayer. While there are several versions it essentially consists of saying, as you inhale:

Jesus Christ, Son of God;
then exhaling:
have mercy on me, a sinner.

The prayer starts on the lips but needs to descend into the heart where it becomes united with its beat. Sometimes I use this mantra:

Sacred Heart of Jesus,
as I inhale and, as I exhale:
have mercy on me.

Gently pray this ten times before resting in the presence of God's merciful Heart. Repeat the process for an allotted time.

All these forms of prayer have three clear purposes. They:

• place the mind in the heart;
• open the heart to God;
• offer a means to deal with distracting thoughts.

Knowing that we are enfolded – abiding – in the heart of God (John 15.4) means that we're to let go of the conscious 'praying self' rather than 'saying' lots of prayers, and allow ourselves to become part of the great ocean of Divine Love. And when the conscious self does intrude with its nagging commentary on life, gently put it behind you where it's out of sight.

As we respond to God's invitation to deepen our prayer, there eventually comes a desire to simplify our lifestyle and the command to love our neighbour will be more insistent. Indeed, it's the test of our prayer, for our love for the God whom we have not seen has always been realized through growth in love for the neighbour whom we have.

✟

KEEP CALM
AND
MEDITATE

The moment when Jesus, on a visit to his friends Martha and Mary, reminded busy Martha that what her sister was doing – sitting at his feet and listening to him – was more important than what she was doing, and is still countercultural and to be encouraged. It cleanses us of the distraction of noise and, together with solitude, provides the means to encounter self in the 'cell' of the heart:

Go to your cell, your cell will teach you everything.[4]

Often people find it helpful to create a small 'prayer corner' in a room – with an icon, crucifix, candle, etc. … or put them out before prayer. Yet despite the way some of us crave being left alone or long for a 'bit of silence', too much can be difficult as this journey into the heart will probably entail facing our inner world where painful memories lie buried. But this invitation to deepen our prayer also opens the possibility that we can be set free from them. I well remember such dark times and valued the help of my spiritual director (as I still do) as with humility – that vital tool as we come to discover the truth of who we are before God – I began to face them, allowing God's compassionate gaze into the deep recesses of my heart.

Solitude and silence provide opportunities to work towards inner conversion, the 'conversion of the heart', to become the person God is creating you to be. In a society that's becoming overly attracted by the sensual and gives little attention to the internal, do we recognize the need to be 'reaching in'? Isn't this one of the most important insights the Church can offer?

Meditation and contemplation

Meditation – engaging the mind and heart in prayer – has been practised by Christians from earliest times. As the Church grew, many of them moved into the Egyptian deserts and learned the value of silence and solitude. Their prayer often simply consisted of taking a word from Scripture – *Abba*, for example – and gently repeating it beneath their breath until it entered their hearts. You'll find some ways of developing prayer in Appendix 2.

Prayer is not a matter of thinking a great deal, but of loving a great deal.[5]

Contemplation is about growing in love by seeing with the eye of the heart and recentring our own into that of Christ. God will use the desire we have for that Divine encounter by working with us to change us. The way we seek to give undistracted attention to God involves giving ourselves to a simple desire to 'let God be God' in our hearts, and wanting to lose ourselves in God, as a fish in water. It is the heart's silent attentiveness to the One who loves us.

Teresa of Avila, the great Spanish mystic, used the image of the silkworm to illustrate the effect of prayer on the soul. As it develops, it begins to want to be detached from its surroundings which no longer hold interest for it and it spins a cocoon as the process of transformation begins. So it is with the soul as it seeks to grow and becomes enfolded in Christ in this process of becoming a new creation.

This form of prayer isn't for the sake of oneself alone, nor to simply give us pleasurable feelings (such prayer is accompanied by a gradual loss of pleasurable feelings), it's to deepen the conversion of the heart to the Reign of God. It concerns an equally deepening desire to serve God in the ways Jesus reveals.

Seeing God in all things

St Francis saw God in all things and, realizing their inter-relatedness, shows us that we need to develop a heart which looks beneath the outer world and a profound respect for the Earth. His commitment to keeping his heart from being set upon anything other than God is a reminder that the 'prayer of the heart' concerns this refusal to let anything get in the way of God.

St Francis also had a profound desire to be united to Christ to the point that he experienced the effects of the crucifixion (the Stigmata), a powerful reminder that we, too, are called to let Christ form in our hearts. He and his close friend St Clare discovered that by contemplating the figure of Christ crucified their hearts became united with his.

Holy hour

'Holy hour' is a period when the Blessed Sacrament is exposed on an altar. The process of my conversion was greatly helped as I knelt, with others, before Jesus present in the consecrated Host:

> O Christ, whom now beneath a veil we see,
> may what we thirst for soon our portion be,
> to gaze on thee unveiled, and see thy face,
> the vision of thy glory and thy grace.[6]

Churches would benefit from giving attention to the place where the Blessed Sacrament is reserved and encourage people to stop and pray there.

> What wonderful majesty! What stupendous condescension! O sublime humility! That the Lord of the whole universe, God and the Son of God, should humble

*Himself like this under the form of a little bread, for our
salvation ... In this world I cannot see the Most High
Son of God with my own eyes, except for His Most Holy
Body and Blood.*[7]

Use your imagination

A couple of hundred years after Francis' death, a man was
born in Spain whose spirituality still has much to teach us – St
Ignatius of Loyola.

Used to reading novels, he found a more lasting sense of
satisfaction after reading the Gospels, or daydreaming about
the lives of the saints, and developed a form of prayer that
uses the imagination. Many find that praying with the Scriptures, using our senses to imagine ourselves in Gospel scenes
– the heat of the day, noise of crowds, smell of water, touch
of a hand on skin or sight of Jesus as he speaks to an individual – connects us more deeply with the movements of the
Spirit in our hearts as we seek to be open to the Word of
God. Ignatius developed this form of prayer to assist those
who wanted to understand how God might be calling them
and the Spiritual Exercises he devised (a focused, processed
time of prayer spent at a Religious House or during a retreat
in daily life) are still valued.

ॐ

English spirituality

Among the great works that can help our spiritual growth,
two books from the English tradition stand out.

The Cloud of Unknowing, a short work by an unknown
medieval writer, says that the essence of prayer is to 'Lift up
your heart to God with humble love: and mean God himself

and not what you can get out of him.'[8] The author goes on to say that, because a thick cloud of 'unknowing' shields us from the bright gaze of God, we need to pierce it with the 'sharp darts of longing love'.

Revelations of Divine Love is by Julian of Norwich who lived in the fifteenth century. She received a number of 'showings' concerning the depths of God's love. Rooted in the Passion of Christ, Julian writes of the Motherhood of Christ, the place of Mary and the way we're enclosed in Love.

The goal of our praying

In the end this matter of human-being is all about how we reach out to the Other, which is what prayer is all about. I pray because I need to; I don't pray to 'get' something out of it but because, in the deepest recesses of my heart, I need to be open to God. It can often feel dry and empty and I spend most of the time dealing with a hundred and one distractions. But I know I must be there because, just when I am not expecting it, a door to heaven opens.

Come as a flame and, like unto the wind,
come from the heights of heaven,
Holy Spirit of God.
Touch our tongues, illuminate our minds,
make our hearts strong when we need you most.
Give us to think of you,
help us to worship you,
please lead our hearts to you,
O God, the Holy Spirit. Amen.
(Source unknown)

ॐ

Invitation:

Pray with the name 'Jesus' for at least five minutes: breathe the name into your heart and 'watch' it descend. If you're distracted, gently let go of the distraction and return to the word. Rest with it in your heart.

Notes

1 From *Story of a Soul*, trans. Fr John Clarke OCD, © 1975, 1976, 1996, Washington Province of Discalced Carmelites. Washington, ICS Publications, pp. 242–3. www.icspublications.org

2 *Seeking God Within*, St Margaret Mary SPB.

3 There are a number of books about the Rosary including: Br Tom Schultz OHC, *The Rosary for Episcopalians/Anglicans*, Regent Press, 2012.

4 Abba Moses the Black (fourth century), *Sayings of the Desert Fathers*.

5 E. W. Truman Dicken, *Teresa of Jesus and John of the Cross*, New York, OUP, 1936, pp. 363–76.

6 St Thomas Aquinas, 1225–1274.

7 St Francis of Assisi, *Letter to a General Chapter*.

8 *The Cloud of Unknowing* (author unknown, fourteenth century), Penguin Classics, 2001, ch. 3.

Chapter 11

For reflection and discussion

- How would you define prayer?
- How might you use your body in prayer?
- In what ways might practices of 'everyday contemplation' be of help to you?
- Christ is present in all things. How might you live with greater thankfulness?

12

Abide in Christ

'I am the true vine, and my Father is the vine-grower.
He removes every branch in me that bears no fruit.
Every branch that bears fruit he prunes
to make it bear more fruit.
You have already been cleansed by the word
that I have spoken to you.
Abide in me as I abide in you.'
John 15.1–4

❧

'What brings you here?' I asked the young woman who appeared at Mass. 'Well,' she replied, 'I read one of your leaflets that dropped through my door and decided to come. There's nothing wrong except I sense there's *more* to life and want to find out what you offer.' We didn't 'offer' much – no clubs, home groups – but she found in our worship something she needed and, eventually, had her children baptized.

The very act of going to church can be daunting for it's not only about entering a strange building, it's an act of unconsciously opening the door to the deep mystery of the Self and seeing that Self reflected in the eyes of God.

The Body of Christ

If you asked most people what the word 'church' meant they'd probably say something about a building, but when the Creed talks about the 'holy catholic church' it isn't talking about a building but a *people* who were encouraged to become holy through the way they lived:

> *All who believed were together and had all things in common; they would sell their possessions and goods and distribute the proceeds to all, as any had need. Day by day, as they spent much time together in the temple, they broke bread at home and ate their food with glad and generous hearts, praising God and having the good-will of all the people. And day by day the Lord added to their number those who were being saved.*
> *(Acts 2.44–47)*

That's quite demanding and, with persecution and growth, gave way to more practical means for the community of believers to arrange its life. Those who felt called to a more radical way of life went into the deserts where they formed small communities that grew into the movement known as the Religious Life (monks, nuns, brothers and sisters).

Jesus had spoken intimately of himself as a vine and his disciples as its branches, telling them to abide in him. Paul refers to the Church as the 'bride' (cf. Eph. 5.25f.) and 'body' (Rom. 12.4–5) of Christ. We are his members called to be united to him, and one another, in bonds of love. Those bonds include worshipping together – especially through the Eucharist where the Body of Christ becomes truly present.

For those who live alone, attending Mass can be one of the few occasions of encountering others to any meaningful extent. I always remember the elderly woman who told me that the Peace was the one occasion when anybody, now, touched her. Christianity is an embodied faith – matter matters for us because it mattered to God; Jesus used material things where bread and wine, water, oil – and touch, communicate the love of God.

As bride and body, the Church exists to help us be *intimate* with God, to grow in at-one-ness with the Divine. Being part of the Church means we're not alone nor simply citizens of an earthly country, we're part of a body that exists in eternity and isn't defined by borders. Christians must stand against petty parochialism and nationalism, and because we *are* part of Christ's Body then wherever a Christian suffers, all suffer – something we need to remember. We mustn't forget the sufferings of our persecuted brothers and sisters, especially in the land called Holy.

Ours is a faith which spread by the preaching of the gospel as Christ's disciples scattered throughout the 'known' world. Tradition tells us that Thomas, for example, went to India, Matthew to 'the East' and Mark to Egypt and the continuing existence of the Church in many of those places is evidence of their endeavours. Their preaching was as much by the way they lived as by the words they spoke – and that must still be the case. People expect to see in us something of what they see in Christ – we're to proclaim the Reign (kingdom) of God through our lives. Believers are to resist the temptation of selfish profit-making and seek to work for the good of all, especially the most vulnerable; show how the welfare of the environment trumps financial wealth; realize the value of all things rather than their cost; consider what we can give back rather than get out of the world. Our attention should be on working for the common good rather than gain.

It's only a crutch

Some will accuse those who go to church of needing a crutch, which can be very painful and cause real difficulties for anyone who wants to grow in their faith and begins to sense that, to do so, they *do* need the company of others. Being human is about finding ourselves in relationship with others and being part of a church is one step along the way, yet we are not to get stuck at that point. The point of 'going to church' is not to find friends, but to be aided on our journey into God.

The building where the people meet is primarily a place of encounter, of meeting, with the mystery of God. Written in gold above the church porch in my last parish were these words: *Hic domus Dei est et porta coeli* – 'This is the house of God and gate of heaven'. The inscription comes from Genesis (28.17) when Jacob encounters God in a dream and, in response, sets up an altar for worship. Of course, we also meet friends but let's not forget that it's a place where we first offer our worship and *then* greet others, especially the stranger in our midst. So some churches have this simple instruction at the door:

> *Speak to God before Mass;*
> *speak to each other afterwards.*

That reflects the ordering of the two great commandments: 'You shall love the Lord your God with all your heart, and with all your soul, and with all your strength, and with all your mind; and your neighbour as yourself' (Luke 10.27). Whatever else we need to do, whoever we might need to greet – and these things may be necessary and good – we're to make the approach to God our priority. To enter a church where people are praying is a moving experience, so when you do, be still for a while, kneel in silence and focus into Christ – *that's* the first move into prayer.

Holy and catholic

At every ordination, the bishop states: 'The Church of England is part of the One, Holy, Catholic and Apostolic Church worshipping the one true God, Father, Son and Holy Spirit.' I remember being a bit confused when I first came across the word 'catholic' in the Creed and wondered if that meant

Roman Catholic but then discovered it means universal and indicates an understanding of the Christian Faith that's been accepted down the centuries. 'Roman' Catholic is the way that Faith has been developed in that part of the Church centred on Rome.

Some think that the Church of England, with the monarch as Supreme Governor, was founded by Henry VIII. But they're only the 'governor' of the earthly Church whose head is Christ. The Church affirms its continuity with the first Christians in Britain, which is why the Archbishop of Canterbury is in unbroken succession to St Augustine, sent to England in 597 AD by Pope St Gregory I.

In the early part of the nineteenth century a great 'Catholic Revival' began in the Church of England. Much was recovered that had been lost through the Reformation – Sacramental life with the Eucharist at the heart of worship; the Religious Life and Retreat movement; the wealth of teaching from the early Church about Christian living; an emphasis on social concern and insights into holiness by saints down the ages.

Thanks be to God, throughout the history of the church it has always been clear that a person's perfection is measured not by the information or knowledge they possess, but by the depth of their charity.[1]

This call to grow in holiness isn't about being 'holier than thou' but about living in the love of God and the lifelong process of allowing that love to transform our lives. It's Jesus we look to for an example of holiness and the one thing that stands out about *his* holiness is that it was revealed in a life committed to the love of his Father and fellow human beings. Being holy is a consequence of loving God with *all* your heart and soul – *and* your neighbour as yourself.

Belonging, aloneness – and brokenness

Belonging to this body can address the hardest aspects of the loneliness experienced by some. Ultimately, we *are* all alone, something we either seek to accept or escape from, but if we do accept our aloneness, enter our heart and nurture that place, we find a certain freedom and don't *need* others as a means of escape. Our heart can become a place of hospitality.

However, you may be one of those who enjoy their aloneness and find large groups of people difficult. Many don't feel called to take part in socials, belong to groups, etc., and apart from needing to be nourished through the Sacraments, find their belonging in different ways, connecting, for example, with a religious community or contemplative network.[2]

Sadly, for some the church is not a place of holiness but of abuse. It's the context in which they've been broken – damaged physically, emotionally or spiritually – or the words or actions of 'Christians' have been deeply wounding. The way some exercise power for their own ends or condemn or mistreat people because of their gender or sexuality is shocking, and while many religions can be narrow-minded or homophobic it's often Christianity that's seen to be bigoted.

Our faith isn't exempt from corruption, misuse or a fundamentalist interpretation, but being a Christian doesn't mean you're an extremist. At its best it offers a way of life that can unite us with that which is most noble and creative in our humanity, although it can be, and has been, abused and used as a means of control. There's a 'dark side' to everything; we're all flawed and 'fallen' and Christ weeps in a thousand places, not least over the inhumanity of some in the Church which can prevent people encountering his compassionate love.

But the greater part of Christ's Body is ever-glorious although it bears wounds, wounds through which light can pour allowing us to glimpse a vision of what we might be.

Don't let your life give evidence against your tongue.
Sing with your voices ... sing also with your conduct.[3]

&

Worship

Worship lies at the heart of the Church, but what is it? Usually connected with what's done in church, some consider worship can be measured by the extent to which our feelings are moved. I recall finding myself in floods of tears during Mass at the Shrine of St Francis because this man – the 'Poverello of Assisi' – speaks to me so powerfully of Christ.

Religion and emotion can be a heady mix, and our view of God will affect our worship. If God is considered a demanding judge that will affect our worship, as will the notion that God is all-loving and compassionate. Worship is about acknowledging and responding to another's worth with all one's heart, soul and mind. It's something we *give*; about directing attention to another; uniting each to the other. It's the duty we owe to God, our sacrifice of thanks and praise which can be silent as well as vocal. As someone wrote to me:

> *I am prepared to stop what I am doing at least once a day, go into a quiet place and give 40 minutes to God. Those 40 minutes are His. It is my sacrifice to Him. It is sacred time. It is consecrated time. What I do during those 40 minutes and what I experience during those 40 minutes is not really the point. The point is that I give Him time and so make a statement of what He is worth to me.*[4]

As the years go by, I notice my feeling for my partner deepening as my love for him matures; feelings are no longer so obviously 'emotional'. There are times when it's just very ordinary – and very challenging. The same happens as our relationship with God matures. It can't be measured by the way feelings are stirred – I now know a deeper desire to be given to the Other, to be abandoned to the One who is all-good; who is love and beauty, mystery and creativity. My relationship is moving beyond a youthful crush to a love which is more pervasive, expressed in my worship of God who is in all things. Worship becomes less about how I feel and more about who I am.

Lift up your heart to God with humble love: and mean God himself and not what you can get out of him.[5]

Being human is about a being who worships, and if someone doesn't worship God, they'll worship something else. To centre our heart on God opens us up to our Godlike being, our 'otherness'. Jesus gave himself to his Father and worshipped him in spirit and truth (John 4.24). He worshipped in solitude, in the Temple where sacrifices were offered and in synagogues where Scriptures were read and set psalms sung to simple melodies. That pattern was followed by the early Church and has given us the Daily/Divine Offices (Morning, Midday, Evening and Night Prayer).

Whatever else we may do in church this pattern feeds us in a way nothing else can and prevents worship becoming dependent on mood. Rooted in practices with which Jesus would have been familiar, worship is the vehicle by which our heart and rational nature join – an inclination of the soul to its maker expressed throughout our lives. For worship doesn't end when we leave the church. In his concluding Address to the Anglo-Catholic Congress of 1923 Bishop Frank Weston said this:

If you are Christians then your Jesus is one and the same: Jesus on the Throne of his glory, Jesus in the

Blessed Sacrament, Jesus received into your hearts in Communion, Jesus with you mystically as you pray, and Jesus enthroned in the hearts and bodies of his brothers and sisters up and down this country. And it is folly – it is madness – to suppose that you can worship Jesus in the Sacraments and Jesus on the Throne of glory, when you are sweating him in the souls and bodies of his children. It cannot be done.

৵

The Sacraments

Our relationship with God is nurtured by the Sacraments, a word meaning to 'make holy'. Defined by the sixteenth-century Anglican theologian Richard Hooker as 'visible signs of invisible grace' there are two 'major' Sacraments – Baptism and the Eucharist – and five others: Confirmation, Anointing of the Sick, Confession, Matrimony and Ordination. Their effectiveness – fruitfulness – doesn't depend on the worthiness of the priest but is the direct work of God in the soul of the one who receives them.

Baptism and Confirmation

We become part of Christ's Body through Baptism in water in the name of the Father and of the Son and of the Holy Spirit. Baptism recalls the way John the Baptist called people to die to their old life and rise to a new way of living and reflects the way Jesus 'passed through' the 'waters' of rebirth – his death and resurrection.

For hundreds of years Baptism was the sacrament of initiation, binding candidates into life in the Trinity. It included being anointed with the oil of chrism (symbolizing the gift of the Holy Spirit) and receiving Holy Communion. Over time, however, Confirmation and First Communion were split from Baptism and, nowadays, children are often prepared for the latter from about the age of seven with Confirmation later. It was common (and still is possible) for a person to take on a new name – usually the name of a saint to whom they commended themselves – to symbolize this new life.

Because you can't be separated from the Body of Christ you can only be baptized once. However, people can reaffirm their baptismal promises, which can be a powerful statement for an individual, something formally repeated at the Easter Eucharist.

> *These three things God requires of all the Baptized:*
> *right faith in the heart, truth on the tongue, temperance*
> *in the body.*[6]

The Eucharist

Here, doing what Jesus told us to do to remember him, we encounter the heart of Christian worship. It isn't just a simple trip down memory lane, but a real *feeding* on the Body and Blood of the crucified, risen Christ – the food that satisfies yet makes you hungrier. Week by week and day by day his sacrifice is celebrated, Christ becomes truly present beneath the forms of bread and wine and we who are part of his Body feed on that Body: you become what you feed upon.

> *If you are the Body and members of Christ,*
> *it is the sacrament of your very self that is placed on the*
> *   Lord's table;*
> *it is the sacrament of your very self you receive.*
> *You answer 'Amen' to what you already are.*[7]

Rooted in the Jewish Passover the Eucharist celebrates the triumph of Christ over death. Time becomes timeless and we're one with those disciples who gathered with Christ in the Upper Room, as they were one with those who celebrated their liberation from slavery in Egypt (Exodus 3.13ff.). This 're-*membering*' does just that – it reconnects us with those events so that, like the Jewish people, 'in each generation, each person is obligated to see themselves as though he or she personally came forth from Egypt'.[8] Though Steve or Mary may preside over the celebration, their vestments – the stole and chasuble – are signs that they do so in the name of Christ.

Christians prepare themselves to take part in this liturgy through prayer and fasting and there are many devotional manuals that can help you get ready to welcome Christ in Word and Sacrament. How bread and wine become the Body and Blood of Christ through the action of the Holy Spirit we cannot know; what we *do* know is that he said: 'This is my body ... my blood...' As Queen Elizabeth I is reputed to have written:

> 'Twas Christ the Word that spake it
> The same took bread & brake it
> And as the Word did make it
> That I believe & take it.

For 2,000 years, Christians have gathered for the Eucharist on Sundays and other Holy Days such as the Ascension to feed on him who is present beneath these outer forms. When we gather we do so as participants, not as audience; we actively pray rather than passively watch. It isn't a performance by priest and servers; we're all actors in this drama. Our eyes need to be drawn by the drama of the Liturgy, not words in a book or on a screen. We're those who stand as willing servants in the presence of God, for here the King of Kings becomes present – bread is his Body, wine his Blood. The

Prayer which we affirm through our 'Amen' (so be it) isn't just a matter of speaking the words of Jesus – it's a prayer that takes us into the great sweep of the story of our creation and re-creation, taking us into heaven as we engage with it:

> The Lord be with you.
> *And also with you.*
> Lift up your hearts [to heaven].
> *We lift them to the Lord [with whom we are present].*
> Let us give thanks to the Lord our God.
> *It is right to give thanks and praise [to the One present to us].*

Though the authors of the Book of Common Prayer (BCP) addressed Reformation controversies, the non-Orthodox world had forgotten the importance of the work of the Holy Spirit, a work only recently rediscovered. The BCP is a work of its time; we now know that the Holy Spirit, invoked on the gifts of bread and wine, animates the 'yeast' of Christ. His sacrifice, once offered, reveals itself whenever we 'do this in memory' of him; and all our sacrifices are gathered into his whenever that sacrifice is re-membered (brought together) before the Father.

Christ comes to us in all his fullness in either the Host or Precious Blood, but some prefer to receive only the former. However, while receiving from the same cup as your sister or brother in Christ is an important sign of our common unity, if you only receive the Host, don't dip it into the chalice (it's called 'intinction') as it can be unhealthy and so is banned by some Anglican Provinces who recommend communion in only one kind (the Host) as the 'best option for those fearful of the cup' (Anglican Church of Canada).

Nor does the Eucharist 'end' when we leave the church; we go with Christ into the world and are called to live 'eucharistically' – 'thankfully'. This ought to be one of our defining characteristics because it has the power to change lives – ours and others. Each day we can grow in this way of living; greeting the world as a gift of God for which we render thanks and praise while offering our lives as a 'living sacrifice'.

Anointing

The Church's Ministry of Healing has always included Anointing with Oil. The Letter of James says that those who are sick should ask for this means of healing (5.14). It's not primarily miraculous but part of a process we engage in that involves the action of God through the health services and prayer. Olive oil (we're rediscovering the value of this for many healing purposes), consecrated by the bishop at the Chrism Mass on Maundy Thursday, is used and if you want to know more, speak to your priest.

Confession

Many think that only Roman Catholics make their confession, but that's not the case: all of us are 'sinners' and there'll be times we need to unburden ourselves. Confession to a priest, through whose ordination Christ gives the privilege of pronouncing Absolution, has always been available to Anglicans and will feature in the section on 'Forgiveness'.

Matrimony

Rooted in Christ's presence at the Wedding Feast at Cana (John 2.1–11), this Sacrament concerns the union of two human beings just as Christ is mystically united to the Church. The priest doesn't 'marry' them, it's the couple who are the ministers of the Sacrament witnessed by the priest who prays a solemn blessing on them. Marriage isn't just about the union of bodies through which we gift ourselves to each other, marriage also reflects the desire of God for union with the soul. That's why it's best celebrated in the context of the Nuptial (Wedding) Mass, for that communion enabled by the Mass addresses the need for the two to become one – not by each consuming the other but by being consumed in love for each other.

> *The Eucharist is the Sacrament of Love;*
> *it signifies Love, it produces love.*
> *The Eucharist is the consummation*
> *of the whole spiritual life.*[9]

Ordination

This involves being called to a pastoral and sacramental ministry whereby the person can be most fully themselves as they seek Christ through either the diaconate or priesthood. Both concern that evangelizing 'love of the Heart of Jesus' and require a considerable amount of humility – it's not about the individual, but about God. And while ministry may involve leadership the diaconate reminds us that the heart of both concerns a desire to *serve* God and people. 'The priesthood', said St John-Mary Vianney, 'is the love of the Heart of Jesus.'

So if you find yourself drawn by the Sacraments and caring for others, take it all into your prayer and make sure you say a strong, 'Not my will but yours be done, O Lord.' For it is the Church that must discern a vocation – all you can do is offer yourself to the process. Talk with your priest if you feel you have that calling.

❧

The Bible

Your word is a lamp for my feet
and a light upon my path.
(Psalm 119.105)

Some see the Bible as some sort of 'instruction manual' but it's not our equivalent to the Quran which Muslims believe is the 'Word of God' (for Christians, that's Jesus). Rather the Bible (a word meaning library, comprising the Old and New Testaments and Apocrypha) witnesses through a collection of writings to the way God has both revealed and been revealed to people. It shows how that story, stormy at times, questioning at others, offers the potential for transformation and fulfilment. It tells of God, with whom we're intertwined, reaching into humanity. Along with the Sacraments, the Scriptures, selected by the Church, offer a means of encountering God's Word and growing into holiness.

It's provided the narrative that's shaped our culture, which challenges much of our 'natural' understanding of what life's about. We're not to demand an eye for an eye (Matt. 5.38–42) but to love our enemies (Matt. 5.43–48); to beware the danger of wealth (Luke 8.14f.), etc. To forget that these basic beliefs are rooted in God's revelation can cause us to be trapped by disordered desires.

The 'Biblical Cycle' and the cycle of the Church's year

If you look at the Bible as a whole, you'll see there's a narrative flowing through it:

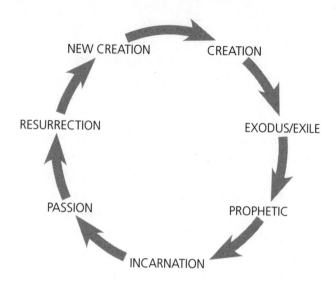

This 'Cycle' informs what's called the 'Church's Year', which takes us from Advent (waiting and watching), through Christmas (the revelation of the Word made flesh), Ordinary Time (when little seems to happen, yet the Word is at work), Lent (preparing and stripping) to Easter and the glories of the age to come (Pentecost). This cycle is dynamic and reminds us that joy and suffering are a necessary aspect of what it means to be alive. It weaves in and out, expressing life's mystery and revealing its treasures. Each 'book' is full of metaphors, some being far richer in mystery than others and we'll need to engage our heart as well as our head. To look for literalism is to miss the point, and the point is not to prove things but to gain deeper wisdom which, for Christians, is discovered most clearly in Jesus, the Word incarnate.

The person who thirsts for God eagerly studies and meditates on the inspired Word, knowing that there he is certain to find the One for whom he thirsts.[10]

As a child, I remember my grandmother reading her Bible each evening, something that seemed odd to me then, but which I now know to be vital in the life of a Christian. As to which version to read, choose a recent translation (e.g. NRSV or NJB) for the Word was uttered in plain speech (John 16.29), not shrouded in antiquated, if romantic, language.

The Old Testament

What we call the Old Testament is a collection of documents put together by a group of Jewish rabbis. It includes the Torah (Genesis to Deuteronomy), the Prophets and other writings such as the Psalms which were known to Jesus, so when the Bible refers to the 'Scriptures' it's referring to these.

The Psalms

The Psalms express every human emotion: awe and wonder, sadness and fear, love, hate, thanksgiving, joy and hope. They're full of sorrow too because, being aware of the Love that enfolds us, they acknowledge, in the eyes of the One who desires us, the truth of who we are – beloved sinners.

Because of all this they've played a central part in the Daily/Divine Office. Many find that taking time to pray a short Office each day is a helpful aid to prayer as it stills the heart, soaking it with the words of the psalms which have nurtured people in their relationship with God for thousands of years:

O God, you are my God; at dawn I seek you;
for you my soul is thirsting.
For you my flesh is pining,
like a dry, weary land without water.
I have come before you in the sanctuary,
to behold your strength and your glory.
(Psalm 63.1–2)

The Apocrypha

The Apocrypha is a fascinating collection of ancient Jewish writings that have certain affinities with the various books of the Old Testament but weren't approved by Christians as a whole. The Old Testament Apocrypha (e.g. Tobit, Judith, Ecclesiasticus, etc.) contains important writings which are accepted by many churches. There are, probably, other documents now lost beneath the sands of the desert that helped shape the Church in lands now regarded as Islamic, which had churches under local bishops, including in China, but whose Christian heritage has been obliterated.

The New Testament

The New Testament comprises three similar gospels, Matthew, Mark and Luke, and that of John telling the life of Christ; an account of the Acts of the Apostles; the Letters of Paul and others; and that work which almost didn't get included – Revelation. Some assume Paul was one of the disciples – but he only encountered Jesus after the Resurrection (Acts 9), an event that's worth reading about. For a long time, Letters (Epistles) were circulated and stories about Jesus were shared by word of mouth before being written down. Many documents were rejected by the Church although some which had been in existence before Christ (the Apocrypha) are accepted by the mainstream churches.

You might have come across the term 'Bible believing' but this often masks sexual or gender prejudices. Jesus would have roundly condemned those who use the term to support, for example, homophobic views (cf. Matt. 23.15) and parables like that of the Good Samaritan show how he challenged prejudice. No matter how 'broad' Anglicanism may be, such views, which give oxygen to persecution, must be resisted. They can have no place in the Church and those

who promote them bear responsibility for the suffering that
can ensue.

అ

The Religious Life

The other way in which people talk about vocation is in rela-
tion to Religious Life. Almost extinguished in the Church of
England at the Reformation, it was refounded in the mid-
nineteenth century and now comprises both apostolic (active)
and monastic/contemplative congregations for men and
women.

People who sense a more radical call to follow the way of
Christ find that the Vows of Poverty, Chastity and Obedience
enable them to grow in Christ. Benedictine, Franciscan,
Carmelite, Augustinian and other spiritualities inform the
Life and there are also groups of married and single people
in Third Orders, Oblatures and different forms of Religious
Life.

This vocation is vital for the health of the Church and
needs support and encouragement. Its radical nature should
act as a reminder of its call to the rest of the Church, which is
diminished without it. Our present overactive culture needs
those who remind us of the fundamental importance of a
balanced life of prayer and action. We need contemplatives
as never before.

The Religious Life, seemingly peripheral, is at the heart of
the life of the Body for it is a life totally consecrated to union
with God – perhaps you are called in this way?

Creator God,
you invite us to share in the life of your Son
and nourish us with his Body and Blood.
May we reveal his presence in all we do and say,

live with ever-deepening thankfulness
and give glory to you,
Father, Son and Holy Spirit. Amen.

❧

Invitation:

Reflect over your day, be present to it in its different parts.
Try praying 'I offer thanks and praise' for each aspect of your
day. How does that affect the way you view it?

Notes

1 Pope Francis, *Gaudate et Excultate*, 3 © Libreria Editrice Vaticana.

2 There's a network of people in the Church of England who feel
called to the single life: www.singleconsecratedlife-anglican.org.uk

3 St Augustine of Hippo, Sermon 34.

4 Peter Dixon TO.SSF.

5 *The Cloud of Unknowing*, ch. 3.

6 St Gregory Nazianzen (329–390). Sr Benedicta Ward SLG, *Sayings
of the Desert Fathers*, 1, 45.

7 St Augustine, Sermon 272.

8 Haggadah text for the Passover.

9 St Thomas Aquinas, *Summa Theol.* IIIa, q. 73, a.3.c.

10 St Bernard of Clairvaux, *Commentary on the Song of Songs*,
Jazzybee Verlag, 2016, 23:3.

Chapter 12

For reflection and discussion

- What is the purpose of 'going to church'?
- Read one of the Gospels (Mark's is the shortest). What stands out for you?
- Reflect on each of the seven Sacraments – why are they important?
- Jesus told us that, in celebrating the Eucharist, he would be present. In what ways might you deepen your devotion to Christ present in the Sacrament?
- In the Eucharist, we are united with Christ's sacrifice of himself. In what ways might his sacrifice inform the way we are to live?

13

Mirrors of God

One should not wish to become a saint in four days
but step by step.
St Philip Neri *(1515–1595)*

☙

The invitation to write this book came when I arrived in Walsingham, Norfolk to begin a retreat. It's a pilgrimage centre, known around the world as 'England's Nazareth', and is home to a replica of the Holy House where Gabriel encountered Mary and invited her to bear the Son of God. I was staying with Sisters whose spirituality is Mary's 'fiat', her 'let-it-be-to-me', and so the seed of what this book concerns – faith in Christ – began to germinate in a place dedicated to Gabriel's message to Mary, Queen of the Saints, who became pregnant with eternity and who can take us deeper into the heart of Christ.

What is a saint?

Saints are the mirrors of God; those through whom Divinity shines like a beacon in the dark, and all who are seeking to love God and neighbour are called to be saints (1 Cor. 1.2). You may know some very saintly people – not necessarily very 'religious' people but those who especially reveal the love of God. There are millions of them – hidden saints who can help us on our own journey of faith. I wonder if you've ever read the life of a saint? Back in the sixteenth century St Ignatius Loyola did, and his life was changed. To know they're close to us and that we can ask their prayers helps to make the 'Communion of Saints' feel very close and homely.

But their popularity in our culture risks being replaced by 'celebrities' whose instant glow through the pages of magazines gives them an immediate, but passing, appeal. True holiness, which takes us out of ourselves so that we encounter the light of the Other, lasts and can be savoured long after a saint has disappeared from this earth.

In the church of St Gregory of Nyssa in San Francisco there's a monumental fresco around its walls of dancing saints. Some are expected – Joseph, Catherine of Siena, Florence Nightingale for example; others not so – Anne Frank, Rumi (the Sufi mystic) – 90 women and men who reveal aspects of glory. The notion of saints is recognized by most religions and even those who wouldn't call themselves Christians might say of someone who'd shown kindness – 'Oh, you're a real saint.' It's a word rooted in the notion that the aroma of God pervades a person even though they won't be aware it does; saints have a sense of humility and don't take themselves too seriously. But what makes a saint and why does the Creed bother to speak about them?

Called to be a saint

'A saint is a sinner who keeps trying.' It's not easy to follow Christ; we make mistakes and face times when we're tempted to give up on the journey. We become tepid or think it's all up to us and forget God. That's normal. Then, as in the account of the Prodigal Son, a little voice speaks in our heart encouraging us to come to our senses and turn back to God. To keep trying because God doesn't give up on us.

Though we're called to be saints, some, whose lives are recognized to be an example to others, are named. In the Roman Catholic Church the process to identify a saint is long and detailed. There must be evidence that the person lived with a depth of faith, hope and love, and that at least two miracles have occurred in response to people asking for their prayers. In other words, their lives were full of grace. It's not as rigorous in the Church of England but it still needs to be clear that the candidate's life is marked by deep faith, trust in God and love for others.

St Paul often addresses his letters to 'the saints' because those who had decided to begin a new way of life by following Christ were setting an example to the world around them. Apart from those recognized by the Church, there is

> ... *a great multitude that no one could count, from every nation, from all tribes and peoples and languages, standing before the throne and before the Lamb, robed in white, with palm branches in their hands.*
> *(Revelation 7.9)*

A rich variety of saints – women, men and children – who've done great works for the benefit of others – teachers, doctors, founders of Religious Orders, etc. Some have died for their faith, and their example can be very moving. From the hundreds of early Christian martyrs to the Franciscan priest, Maximillian Kolbe, who volunteered to replace a young father in a group being starved to death in Auschwitz, and those killed by Isis for not renouncing their faith, the story of Christianity is that it has been 'the blood of the martyrs which is the seed of the church'.[1]

That's why red vestments are worn on the feast of martyrs (a word meaning 'witness'). Others, who haven't been killed for their faith, but whose witness to Christ speaks powerfully, are known as 'white martyrs'. Such people can be equally impressive, especially when they stand up against corruption, injustice and oppression.

Holy living

It's not quite true that there's no DIY manual about being a saint – Jesus' teachings contain our instructions. Saints are made in the fires of life, in darkness and difficulty, emerging in society when we need them.

> *Be brave! Let's remember our duty and perform it with-out complaint. There will be a way out. God has never deserted our people. Through the ages Jews have had to suffer, but through the ages they've gone on living, and the centuries of suffering have only made them stronger.*[2]

The Cistercian monk, Thomas Merton (1915–1968), said that the call to be a saint was the same as the call to 'be yourself'. He didn't mean we don't need to bother struggling with our faults and failings, far from it. What we need is to become the people we are in the sight of God, to be true to our calling, to let go of whatever distracts us from being the glorious creation God intends. Such humility is the bedrock of sanctity. It's about being real – knowing ourselves through the eyes of God. Many of us feel embarrassed when we're praised for what we've done. It can be like having a torch shone on a door behind which lies something we find difficult to relish. At such times, try rejoicing in that good thing and heed St Francis' advice in his First Rule: 'Render to God all that is good.' Saints show us what it can be like to be fully human.

> *Young people of every continent, do not be afraid to be the saints of the new millennium! Be contemplative, love prayer; be coherent with your faith and generous in the service of your brothers and sisters, be active mem-bers of the Church and builders of peace. To succeed in this demanding project of life, continue to listen to His*

Word, draw strength from the Sacraments, especially the
Eucharist and Penance. The Lord wants you to be intrepid
apostles of his Gospel and builders of a new humanity.[3]

Each of us is called to be a saint, to live holy lives. Apart from
the converting power of the Sacraments of the Eucharist and
Confession, the Beatitudes (Matt. 5.3–11), read as the Gospel
for the Feast of All Saints (1 November), show us the way:
'Blessed are the pure in heart for they shall see God.'

Our friends in heaven

However, in light of this call there are times when, for no
apparent reason, I find myself on the edge of a well of inner
darkness, a sense that can continue for some days. To realize the love of my partner and have the company of friends
is a real help, but there's a way I also need to recall that
I'm one with the saints. They surround me and enfold me;
in the Body of Christ, I am one with them, bound into that
great company of holy ones – with John the Divine, Cuthbert,
Hildegard and all who have gone before who have sought to
love God. To be a Christian isn't just about belonging to the
Church on earth, it's about being part of the timeless Body of
Christ which exists on earth *and* in heaven.

When we celebrate the Eucharist it's not just those visibly
gathered who are present; we're one with angels and archangels and all the company of heaven. Time was when the
walls of our churches, like St Gregory's now, were covered in
frescoes of saints to remind people they weren't alone. Now
that's not normally the case, but we need to recall, as we
celebrate, that we stand with saints and angels worshipping
before the throne of God. These are the people we look to
who show us how to live.

He will provide the way and the means, such as you could never have imagined. Leave it all to Him, let go of yourself, lose yourself on the Cross, and you will find yourself entirely.[4]

Holy places and pilgrimage

Pilgrimage to a place where a saint has lived, died or appeared is important to Christianity because of the way we're called to be journeying in our faith. The world is full of such 'thin places' (like Walsingham) where heaven seems close, veiled only by gossamer. To pray in the cell of Dame Julian in Norwich is to sense her presence, though she died in 1416, encouraging us to be on the move deeper into the mystery of God. We need to turn from the world we know and open our heart to another where the saints dwell in glory. Sometimes that can be a bit unnerving; we don't want to leave the comfort of where we are for something we're unsure about. At other times we have a taste of what's to come and then long for an ongoing encounter.

This call to 'let go and let God' has echoed down the ages. From Abram's response to a call to leave his home for an unknown destination (Genesis 12) to Mary's angelic encounter and *her* response, we're invited to grow beyond ourselves. Walsingham, and of course the Holy Land, invites us to embark on this journey; here the Divine breaks in, sacramental places opening our inner eye to a mystical reality. I remember when, leading a young adult pilgrimage to monasteries in Egypt, we began to play a simple children's game with one of the monks. As it progressed, and we laughed at our antics, I suddenly felt I'd touched something heavenly, a moment filled with Godly friendship, and didn't want it to end.

Venerating the saints

Some worry about the 'worship' of saints; that kissing relics or lighting candles at their shrines detracts attention from God. But it's very natural to want to show respect to good people, to venerate the memory of those whose lives have helped ours. We erect statues of some and display pictures of others – we probably have photos of those we love in our homes which we might kiss at times. A church without a picture or statue of a saint is a bit like a home without the physical memorials of loved ones. And that's what saints are, our loved ones in Jesus to whom we show honour, whose lives offer us an example of Godly living.

Asking for the prayers of Mary and the Saints

Finally, if we realize that the saints are one with us in the Body of Christ that means we can ask for their prayers – especially, the prayers of Mary. She who was a 'feather on the breath of God' was animated by that relationship. She who was 'full of grace' was at one with the Divine Will and it's in that Will we're invited to live. She who is close to the throne of God knows our struggles and fears, hopes and sadness, joys and sorrows and, like a mother, will pray for her children who turn to her in faith and hope and love. May all the saints of God pray for us!

> Hail, holy Queen, Mother of mercy,
> hail, our life, our sweetness and our hope.
> To thee do we cry, poor banished children of Eve:
> to thee do we send up our sighs,
> mourning and weeping in this vale of tears.
> Turn then, most gracious Advocate, thine eyes of mercy
>   toward us,

and after this our exile, show unto us the blessed fruit of
thy womb, Jesus,
O merciful, O loving, O sweet Virgin Mary!

Invitation:

Read a short life of a saint – Francis, Thérèse of Lisieux, Josephine Butler, for example. What do you learn from them?

Notes

  1 Tertullian, *Apologeticus*, 50.
  2 Anne Frank, 11 April 1944, ©ANNE FRANK FONDS, Basel, Switzerland.
  3 Pope St John Paul II, 'Message for World Youth Day', 2000.
  4 From a letter of St Catherine of Siena.

14

Be Reconciled

In failing to confess, Lord,
I would only hide you from myself,
not myself from you.
St Augustine, Confessions 10.2

❧

It was a hot afternoon and I was sitting in the grounds of the Church of Our Lady of the Ark of the Covenant in Kiryat Ye'arim near Jerusalem. I'd just presided at Mass for a group of pilgrims when one approached me with a question that had troubled her for more than 40 years. She was unable to forgive her sister who had upset another member of her family. The incident festered and there, so near to Jerusalem, the words of the Our Father, 'forgive us our trespasses as we forgive those who trespass against us', reopened the pain of that slight.

She'd heard people on television who, having experienced the murder of their child, say that they forgave the perpetrator. Often, they were Christians and she was deeply troubled because of not being able to forgive her sister; the insult still weighed heavily on her heart. As she talked, I reminded her that Jesus only asks us to pray that we might forgive those who sin against *us*. We cannot forgive *x* for the wrong they do to *y*. It's not in our power to do so for we're not the subject of the wrong. But it helps to forgive if we know we're also sinners in need of forgiveness.

Forgiveness

Throughout the Gospels, Jesus insists on the importance of forgiveness. He tells Peter that forgiveness must be limitless (Matt. 18.22), reminds us that our being forgiven depends on us doing likewise (Matt. 6.14) and says that people need to forgive anyone they've a grudge against (Mark 11.25). This hard matter of forgiveness is central to his teaching.

Jesus often tells stories about forgiveness and reconciliation – like the Return of the Prodigal Son (Luke 15.11ff.) or forgiving debt (Matt. 18.23ff.) – and tells us to 'Love your enemies, do good to those who hate you, bless those who curse you, pray for those who abuse you' (Luke 6.27–28). And all because of that new commandment of Jesus – that you love one another. 'Just as I have loved you, you also should love one another' (John 13.34). This is all about changing our *heart* so we don't harbour anger, bitterness, fear and so on. We might pay a lot of money to change our appearance, to make us more attractive, but as someone said to me, 'We may have perfect bodies, but who will forgive me my sins?'

> *Long-suffering and readiness to forgive curb anger;*
> *love and compassion wither it.*[1]

A person who does not repent cannot bear the fruits of forgiveness or find reconciliation, but the heart which forgives is a place of new life. One of the ways that this can be done is to direct a prayer, such as this, towards the object of our hatred: 'May N. be filled with your compassion, Lord; may your love enfold them.' In the end, it's God alone who can forgive sin yet the path to our sanctification requires us to practise God-like acts and learn how to cultivate reconciliation.

Anger

If not addressed appropriately anger can have a corrosive effect on whoever carries it and those connected to them. Think about it – doesn't it often take less energy to love and forgive than to stay angry and hold a grudge? We need to forgive not just for the benefit of the other, but because it sets us free of anger's burden, a burden that can be enormous.

Anger is the Door, by which all Vices enter the Soul.[2]

Reconciliation

'In Christ God was reconciling the world to himself', wrote St Paul (2 Cor. 5.19) so that ultimate reconciliation, between the Divine and human, is the heart of our faith. We're called to be people involved with reconciliation, and not just between individuals; reconciling families, communities and nations is equally important.

In 1914 Christians founded the Fellowship of Reconciliation, an international movement committed to active nonviolence as a way of life and as a means of personal, social, economic and political transformation. At the close of World War Two, Brother Roger Schütz, a Protestant pastor, began a community to offer the means for people to learn to live together. Now based at Taizé in France its members come from different churches and nations and thousands are attracted each year both to that place and to its annual international gatherings.

Christ is communion ... He did not come to earth to start one more religion, but to offer to all a communion in God ... 'Communion' is one of the most beautiful names of the Church.[3]

Desmond Tutu, when Anglican archbishop of Cape Town, also realized the need to help people live together. At the end of the dehumanizing period of apartheid he assisted in the development of the Truth and Reconciliation Commission to heal a profoundly divided society:

> *A person is a person through other persons; you can't be human in isolation; you are human only in relationships.*[4]

He realized that it's only when we face the truth of who we are as a society and as individuals that we can begin to truly grow. This is what we understand to lie at the heart of the Sacrament of Reconciliation/Confession. In the face of so much dogmatism – political, personal and religious – Christians need to be seeking to reconcile rather then divide; to be generous in judgements and hospitable to the other. The faults they might see in others 'must be subjects for prayer rather than criticism and they must be more diligent to take the log out of their own eye than the speck out of their neighbour's (Matt. 7.5)'.[5]

༄

Confession

Ever since the dawn of Christianity the place of forgiveness in the Christian life has been stressed. Baptism cleanses us of sin but doesn't stop the sinning and this Sacrament has long been part of the ministry of the Church because sin, unforgiven, has a corrosive effect. We must be prepared to forgive 'seventy-seven times' (Matt. 18.22), for Christianity teaches that no matter what you've done or how lost you may feel, God will receive you back. The world may offer a critical glare because you've messed up again, but own your fault, ask forgiveness and desire not to sin again.

At the end of John's Gospel, when Jesus appeared to his disciples on the evening of the day of Resurrection, he said to them: 'Receive the Holy Spirit. If you forgive the sins of any, they are forgiven them; if you retain the sins of any, they are retained' (John 20.22–23). This verse has been understood to give authority to absolve those who repent and seek forgiveness. Yet this Sacrament, so embedded in the gospel of Jesus, is one of the Church of England's best-kept secrets (along with the existence of the Religious Life). Though ordination gives every priest this authority, not all wish to hear confessions and not all Anglicans are made aware of the benefits of this grace-filled Sacrament. Yet the Book of Common Prayer advises a person to confess to a priest 'if he feel his conscience troubled with any weighty matter'.[6] Sadly the maxim: 'All may; none must; some should' has often become 'don't bother ...'

Making your confession

There are many ways to make your confession – formally and informally, using set words or direct from the heart – but whatever the way the admission of sins, penitence and a desire not to repeat them is essential. Confession offers a way of owning our faults and offering them to Christ for healing; we are sinners seeking to be made whole.

Traditionally the penitent (the person making their confession) kneels before the priest who encourages them: 'The Lord be in your heart and on your lips that you may rightly and truly confess your sins, in the name of the Father, and of the Son + and of the Holy Spirit'. Making your confession – being open and honest – may be a blessing in disguise, but it's a costly blessing. After all, sin has a price. With such encouragement the penitent begins to open their heart:

I confess to almighty God,
and before the whole company of heaven,
that I have sinned through my own fault,
in my thoughts and in my words,
in what I have done and in what I have failed to do.[7]

We acknowledge the 'whole company of heaven' because sin isn't only a personal matter between you and God; it disrupts the fabric of the universe. In order to right our relationships with the world around us we need to get it right with God and that's where this Sacrament is so helpful.

I've always noticed that to say 'sorry' to God in the presence of another human being has a different effect on me than if I simply do so in my heart, for I must face the truth of my sin when it's out there, in the open (as it were). In the earliest days of Christianity people did make 'open confessions', which is fine providing we're all compassionate human beings who keep confidences. But ... you can imagine what began to happen, and very quickly it was realized that the practice needed to change. Confession became a matter dealt with between 'penitent' and priest, who was bound by strict rules of confidentiality. Even today the 'Seal of the Confessional' cannot, by law, be broken – what's said there stays there. This requirement of absolute confidentiality applies even if matters of grave concern are admitted, unless the confessor's own life is at risk.

Knowing all this, the penitent will then admit their sins ending with words such as:

For these and all the other sins that I cannot remember
I am heartily sorry, firmly mean to do better,
most humbly ask pardon of God and of you,
    Father/Mother,
penance (advice) and absolution. Amen.[8]

Sorrow for what we've done and a real desire to amend one's life must be part of the process. Confession isn't just about finding forgiveness; it's also about desiring to change – part of the conversion process.

Absolution

We've laid it all out before God in the presence of another human being who, in their priestly role, is motivated by the compassion of Christ. If you've asked for 'advice' they'll sift through what's been said looking for the ways in which God is moving in your life, seeking to affirm these. I've always been amazed by the way my confessors have identified matters needing attention which I may not have recognized. Finally, the confessor will assure the penitent of God's forgiveness:

> *Our Lord Jesus Christ, who has left power to his Church*
> *to absolve all who truly repent and believe in him,*
> *of his great mercy forgive you your offences;*
> *and by his authority committed to me,*
> *I absolve you from all your sins, in the name of the Father,*
> *and of the Son + and of the Holy Spirit. Amen.*
> *Go in peace; the Lord has put away your sins,*
> *and pray for me, a sinner too.*[9]

There's something immensely liberating in those words, 'I absolve you'. It's often felt to me as if a great weight has been removed and, while none of us can be set free from the consequences of our sin, that awful burden of guilt has been lightened. As someone wrote about their First Confession:

> *I began 'Bless me Father, for I have sinned. This is my*
> *first confession.' I then pulled the list of sins out of my*
> *pocket and began reading them. When I got to the second*
> *or third one I began crying, and this made it difficult to*
> *talk. I ended up rushing through my list because I wanted*

to be able to say them all before my crying hindered me from speaking at all. I think the crying was a result of the Holy Spirit bringing me into a state of contrition. I had felt fine before going into the confession, and I never expected I would break down like that. I'm very glad this happened though, and I understand why reconciliation is sometimes referred to as 'the sacrament of tears'.

Tears don't always come and aren't the sign of an 'authentic' confession. Nor is 'making your confession' just about making you feel better, it's about accepting our role in that business of reconciliation. Taking responsibility for our part in reordering the world. Accepting that Christ came to reconcile all things – even me – to God. Confession is part of the Church's healing ministry and is deeply therapeutic.

While the Roman Catholic and Orthodox Churches require their members to make their confession at various times, usually before major festivals or before receiving Holy Communion, the Anglican tradition has taken a different approach. However, making your confession before, for example, Christmas and Easter is a great help in enlivening the reality of these celebrations. And there are many for whom confession is part of their regular spiritual discipline as they seek to develop their relationship with God. All of us carry the burden of anger, guilt and sin which, unless dealt with, can have a deeply damaging effect on individuals and societies. Research into human psychology has shown how important it is to be able to deal with these matters, and making confession part of your life in Christ has many benefits, not least that your relationship with him is deepened as you open your heart and express your desire to be reconciled.

Confession is an act of honesty and courage –
an act of entrusting ourselves, beyond sin,
to the mercy of a loving and forgiving God.[10]

Lord,
grant me a desire
to live at one with all creation.
Let me seek the good of all
and not judge my sisters and brothers.
Help me to be reconciled
and give me the courage to open my heart to you
that, recalling my sins and offences,
I might be forgiven.
I ask this in the name of Jesus. Amen.

Invitation:

Read the Parable of the Loving Father (Luke 15.11–32). What attracts you about the story? Put yourself in the shoes of (a) the Prodigal Son, (b) the Loving Father, (c) the elder son. What do you notice about each person? What is the parable saying to you?

Notes

1 St Thalassios the Libyan (seventh century), from *The Philokalia*.
2 St Jerome, quoted by St Alphonsus Liguori CSsR, *On the Sin of Anger*.

3 Br Roger of Taizé, *Glimmers of Happiness*, GIA Publications, 2007, pp. 89, 92.

4 Bishop Desmond Tutu (source unknown).

5 From the *Principles* SSF, Day 26.

6 Book of Common Prayer 1662, Visitation of the Sick.

7 From a traditional form of Confession.

8 The same.

9 The same.

10 Pope St John Paul II – from a Homily, 14 September 1987.

Chapters 13 and 14

For reflection and discussion

- Do you know any saints? How might you define one? What makes for living a holy life?
- Do you know of any examples of reconciliation? What do they say to you? Is there any way you might get involved?
- Read Psalm 51. What speaks to you? What does it teach about forgiveness?
- How might making your confession be helpful in your Christian life? How might you go about it?

15

We Rise in Him

Alleluia!
There we shall rest and see,
we shall see and love,
we shall love and praise.
Behold what will be at the end without end.
For what other end do we have,
if not to reach the kingdom which has no end?
St Augustine, The City of God, Book XXII, Chapter 30

❧

The Eucharist is over, and I've returned to the Sacristy with the servers for a final prayer: 'May the souls of the departed, through the mercy and love of God, rest in peace,' I say. 'And rise in glory!' is the heartfelt response. Except that's not right: it's not the *soul* that rises in glory but the body. We don't know what *kind* of 'body' that will be (1 Cor. 15.35ff.) but that's what the Creed affirms: 'I believe in the resurrection of the *body* and the life of the world to come.'

After we die

People have always been concerned about what happens after we die; many feel this life isn't the end – that there's more to come – and religion has sought to address that concern in different ways.

Enter eagerly into the treasure house that lies within you, and so you will see the treasure house of heaven – for the two are one and the same, and there is but one single entry into them both. The ladder that leads to the kingdom is hidden within you and is found in your own soul. Dive into yourself and in your soul, you will discover the rungs by which to ascend.[1]

Looking back to the Judaism of Jesus' time (and, of course, Jesus was a Jew) there were several developing views: from the idea that the dead stayed in 'Sheol', a dark place of shadows, to an understanding that God as Creator could bring life out of death. And because God is to be closely identified with justice some argued that the resurrection of those who had lived a good and holy life was assured.

Although many say they want a funeral that's 'not religious' and prefer a secular 'minister' without readings from the Bible or talk of God, I've noticed that many, if not most, talk about hoping to encounter their loved ones after death. But if there *is* an afterlife, what's it going to be like? An extension of this one? How will I 'know' others? Surely, it all depends on God? Among the parables Jesus told was one which addresses what happens after we die. He'd been talking with his disciples about the kingdom of God and spoke (Luke 16.19–31) of a poor man who lay at the gate of the house of a rich man who refused to help him. Both died but while the poor man was carried away to be with Abraham, the rich man ended up in Hades – Sheol/Hell. They were separated by a great gulf because the rich man hadn't helped the poor man while they lived.

Heaven is to be with the angels and saints in communion with God – Father, Son and Holy Spirit – and the way there is by living as Christ lived. His life and death have opened the way for us (Hebrews 10.19ff.) whereas Hell is to be separated from that perfect communion of love.

Purgatory

But most of us don't live perfect lives so the Church taught that, after death, we would find ourselves in a 'middle place' – Purgatory. It's not a place of punishment but of preparation as we're lovingly cleansed (purged) before joining that great company of saints and angels. In Chapter 6 we looked at how, after he died, Jesus went and preached to the dead to set them free, and we continue to remember before God those who have died (2 Macc. 12.44–45) and to offer Mass for those in Purgatory with whom we are united in the whole Body of Christ:

> ... *although death comes to us all,*
> *yet we rejoice in the promise of eternal life;*
> *for to your faithful people life is changed, not taken away;*
> *and when our mortal flesh is laid aside*
> *an everlasting dwelling place is made ready for us*
> * in heaven.*[2]

But the Reformation questioned the 'Romish Doctrine', leaving a stark choice between going straight to Heaven – or Hell. That might appeal to those who like in/out solutions, but does it really speak to the way most of us experience life? God doesn't want any of us to end up in Hell (1 Tim. 2.4) and death offers the possibility of being embraced into the vision of God, but might that not require some preparation?

> *Beloved, we are God's children now; what we will be has*
> *not yet been revealed. What we do know is this: when he*
> *is revealed, we will be like him, for we will see him as he*
> *is. And all who have this hope in him purify themselves,*
> *just as he is pure.*
> *(1 John 3.2–3)*

St John of the Cross (1542–1591) compared the way Christ acts upon the soul with how fire acts on a log of wood, transforming it into itself: this purging, cleansing fire of love prepares us for union with God, a theme the Anglican writer C. S. Lewis later addressed in several of books including *Mere Christianity*. Purgatory prepares us to live in the utter freedom of love, a freedom that might come as a shock to those who find it hard to live in its self-surrender: purge my heart, O God, and make it clean. Or, as another prayer says: 'transform the poverty of our nature by the riches of your grace'. As the afterlife is timeless we can't know how 'long' this will go on: maybe it's a bit like getting ready for a celebration – some need longer than others – but our prayers can help them.

✠ *Rest eternal grant to them, O Lord;*
and let light perpetual shine upon them.

Funerals

So it's good to stipulate in your Will that your funeral is to be celebrated in the context of a traditional Requiem Mass in which the person is commended to God. Held in Christ's sacrificial love we offer them to him in whom we pray they will come to life everlasting, asking that God forgive them their sins as, mirroring their baptism, they are sprinkled with Holy Water.

Wherever God is, there is heaven.[3]

The Commemoration of All Souls on 2 November provides an opportunity to remember all the departed. November is the Month of the Holy Souls, although there's a tradition of offering a monthly Requiem for all the departed, reminding us that the veil between the living and those who have gone before is very thin. We're united with them in a deeply powerful way as we're united in Christ's Sacrifice which opened the way to life with God.

When St Francis of Assisi's life drew to a close, he welcomed Sister Death and, as St Ignatius of Antioch approached martyrdom, it is said he could 'hear within him the voice of the Spirit welling up like living water and whispering the invitation: Come to the Father'.

The Last Judgement

Ultimately there comes a final, Last Judgement (John 5.25ff.) when the dead will be separated out as a shepherd separates sheep and goats (Matt. 25.31ff.). In the Holy Land I discovered that they looked similar; but God knows the difference. Those welcomed to Heaven will have fed the hungry, given drink to the thirsty, clothed the naked, visited the sick ... and the others? Well, we all need that period of preparation in Purgatory, but Jesus is clearly telling us where our attention should be given.

So much depends on the mercy of God and how we've lived, which is why that saying of St John of the Cross – 'at the end of our days we'll be judged by our loving' – is so important.

Thy kingdom come

Jesus talked about this time when the 'kingdom of heaven' (or the 'Reign of God') will come in a parable about wise and foolish bridesmaids (Matthew 25.1–13), reminding us that we need to 'keep awake, for you know neither the day nor the hour'. This is the mysterious 'time' (when time is timeless) when there will come a new Heaven and a new Earth (Rev. 21), the 'New Jerusalem':

I heard a loud voice from the throne saying,
  'See, the home of God is among mortals.
He will dwell with them;
they will be his peoples,
and God himself will be with them;
he will wipe every tear from their eyes.
Death will be no more;
mourning and crying and pain will be no more,
for the first things have passed away.'
And the one who was seated on the throne said,
  'See, I am making all things new.'
(Revelation 21.3–5)

And because we're into a timeless realm, this 'making all things new' is constantly occurring. In a wonderful passage in his Letter to persecuted Christians in Rome (8.18ff.), St Paul said that creation itself waited to be set free from 'bondage and decay'; that the whole world, and human beings, have been 'groaning in labour pains until now' awaiting God's embrace of all things to bring about this New Creation. This is what we hope for – not something we can see (that wouldn't be hope) but something we patiently long for.

Spirit, soul and body

I believe I have a spiritual life and a soul, but how I know my 'self' is through the body I inhabit. Yet death takes away my body – and the bodies of my friends – so how can we know each other? My sensual encounters enable my relationships – I can 'make friends' over the internet but I need to encounter another embodied 'self' if I am to have a real relationship. Even Facebook friends need to tap the keys or speak the words that enable contact.

When Jesus first appeared to his disciples after the Resurrection, he made a point of inviting St Thomas to touch the wounds in his body (John 20.27): whatever happens after death, the essence of who we are – body, soul and spirit – lives on. In his first letter to Christians in Corinth Paul had reflected on their questions of how the dead will be raised, saying:

> *What you sow does not come to life unless it dies. And as for what you sow, you do not sow the body that is to be, but a bare seed, perhaps of wheat or of some other grain. But God gives it a body as he has chosen, and to each kind of seed its own body ... So it is with the resurrection of the dead. What is sown is perishable, what is raised is imperishable. It is sown in dishonour, it is raised in glory. It is sown in weakness, it is raised in power. It is sown a physical body, it is raised a spiritual body. If there is a physical body, there is also a spiritual body.*
> *(1 Corinthians 15.35–44)*

Paul realizes that the 'body' as we think of it – a physical being of flesh, muscle, blood and bones – isn't quite what will be raised. Trained as a Jewish rabbi he seems to be trying to hold together a non-dualistic notion of body and soul, matter and spirit, and today we know that matter and energy can never be destroyed, they only take on other forms.[4] The end of the First Letter to the Thessalonians makes mention of this (5.23) by asking that our 'spirit and soul and body be kept sound' at the final coming of Jesus.

There's a beautiful hymn, 'Light's abode, celestial Salem', sung at festivals of the dedication of a church – the Body of Christ – which captures something of the essence of all this:

> *O how glorious and resplendent,*
> *fragile body, shalt thou be,*
> *when endued with so much beauty,*
> *full of health and strong and free,*
> *full of vigour, full of pleasure*
> *that shall last eternally.*

That's from John Mason Neale's translation of a hymn by St Thomas à Kempis (1380–1471). Neale was an Anglican priest and founder of a Religious community – the Sisters of St Margaret – and à Kempis the author of the great work of Christian spirituality, *The Imitation of Christ*:

> *At the Day of Judgement, we shall not be asked what we have read but what we have done; not how well we have spoken, but how we have lived out of the call to holiness.*[5]

While we have hints as to what that life will be like, the prospect of spending eternity strumming a harp hardly excites me. But what seems certain is this: all the good we long for, all the love we have received and all the joys we have known are as nothing compared to the glory that will be revealed (Rom. 8.18). Heaven is where God is, where love enfolds all, and I can't believe that God would reject anyone who seeks him, whether or not they know Jesus. Who the 'sheep' and 'goats' are is God's business to sort out, not ours, so we pray that none may be lost, that the dead will rest in the peace of Christ and that God's kingdom may come on earth as it is in heaven. For now, you and I are simply faced with the question: do I seek to love Jesus with all my heart, soul, mind and strength, and my neighbour – as myself?

Go forth upon your journey from this world,
O Christian soul;
in the name of God the Father who created you.
In the name of Jesus Christ who suffered for you.
In the name of the Holy Spirit who strengthens you.
In communion with Mary, the blessèd Mother of God,
and with all the saints;
with angels and archangels and all the heavenly host.
May your portion this day be in peace +
and your dwelling in the city of God.
Amen.[6]

❧

Invitation:

Look at an image of a chrysalis and reflect on what it says about resurrection.

Notes

1 St Isaac of Nineveh (c. 613–c. 700), from *The Philokalia*.
2 Eucharist – Preface of the Dead.
3 St Teresa of Avila, *The Way of Perfection*, from The Complete Works, Vol. 3, E. Allison Peers, 1946, p. 115.
4 The Law of Conservation of Energy and Mass.
5 Thomas à Kempis, *The Imitation of Christ*, Penguin Classics, 2013, Book 1, ch. 3.
6 The Proficiscere (a version appears in Common Worship, *Funeral Services*).

16

Life in Christ

I believe so that I may understand.
St Anselm, The Proslogion, 1

&

I still find I sometimes wake up in the morning haunted by the question that opened this book – 'What's it all about?' Although I'm fortunate to have a loving partner and good friends the question comes back: what's *life* all about? And what difference do belief and faith make?

What do you seek?

Life provides so many wonderful things to tempt eye and heart to the extent we're spoilt for choice: arts, sport, myriad forms of entertainment, all offering ways to help us relish life. Yet some still aren't at peace with who they are or find the world an oppressive place.

Left to our own devices life can seem 'boring', so we direct our attention to some mindless game on the iPhone, thus avoiding the only person we'll ever have to live with for the rest of our lives – ourselves. But becoming who we're called to be involves facing aspects of ourselves we may find difficult, and the way of – humility – of self-acceptance is the way to wholeness.

It can be quite disturbing when someone begins to buck the trend or says to themselves – 'Nah, a bottle of wine a night isn't working any more'; 'All that bitching and backbiting's beginning to feel bad'; 'This fast road of success, achievement, wealth – it's emptying "me" – what's it giving "me"?' Then the time comes when all we *thought* we wanted or had been told was necessary for a good life – the beauty treatments, perfect body, holidays to far-flung places (regardless of the cost to the planet), having the latest gadget and so on – feels like chasing after sunbeams. Such things may fill the spaces in life but can distract us from the one thing necessary ...

'*Be still and know that I am God.*'
(Psalm 46.10)

And, in coming to 'know' God, being led to know ourselves more deeply. Finding that life *has* meaning and purpose; that, no matter what happens, I am loved ... by God: once that knowledge enters the heart, and an understanding that God was in Christ seeking to bring the world to wholeness, then things can begin to change:

> ... *the modern world shows itself at once powerful and weak, capable of the noblest deeds or the foulest; before it lies the path to freedom or to slavery, to progress or retreat, to brotherhood or hatred. Moreover, man is becoming aware that it is his responsibility to guide aright the forces which he has unleashed, and which can enslave him or minister to him.*[1]

Peace and anxiety

However, many regard religion as simply an escape. Perhaps you live or work in a noisy, hyperactive environment and are one of those people who say, 'I just want to find some peace.' But, maybe, that disturbance is caused by something deeper – warfare in the heart – an inability to let go of fears and anxieties. Or we might find thoughts such as, 'She's always talking about me', 'They're out to take over', 'He has all the luck' beginning to run riot. To bring peace to our hearts, to begin to change them, heed the words of St Dorotheus of Gaza (505–c. 565):

> Do not seek to know about the evil of your neighbour, and do not harbour suspicions against him. If your malice does give birth to suspicions, try to transform them into good thoughts.

There's also a simple prayer we can use to change the way we give attention to the other:

> May you be well;
> may you be happy;
> may you know the compassion of Christ.[2]

When our hearts are disturbed, we need to learn to be detached from the associated feelings and not give them our attention – notice, but let them go and, if they return, hand them to God. Look over their shoulder to God's compassionate gaze. If they keep returning, then ask God to help you understand their cause – maybe with the help of a spiritual director. There's a prayer which can be used at the end of the Our Father at Mass that speaks into this need:

> Deliver us, Lord, from every evil,
> and grant us peace in our day.
> In your mercy keep us free from sin
> and protect us from all anxiety
> as we wait in joyful hope for the coming
> of our Saviour, Jesus Christ.

Learn to be compassionate towards yourself. Accept that you are the beloved of God who looks upon you with mercy. And live in the present moment, don't be trapped by what has happened; you can't change the past and it's exhausting to worry about a future over which you've little control: 'do not worry about your life, what you will eat or what you will drink, or about your body, what you will wear ... if God so clothes the grass of the field, which is alive today and tomorrow is thrown into the oven, will he not much more clothe you – you of little faith?' (Matthew 6.25–30).

જ

Baptismal Life

Vocation

From the start we're being 'called' by God into a deeper, loving relationship. Not called audibly but something our hearts hear just as Mary heard the angel inviting her to become the Mother of God.

We're all called to be changed into the person God is calling us to become – that's our vocation – though often when people talk about 'vocation' they mean a calling to the priesthood or Religious Life. In listening to God some *will* sense a draw to give their lives as monks, nuns, religious brothers or sisters (and there are many religious communities in the Anglican Communion). But deeper than this there's a 'personal vocation' which identifies who I am and invites my response. St Thérèse of Lisieux realized hers when she read 1 Corinthians 13 and 14 and exclaimed, 'My vocation is to love!' This calling will echo deep in our heart and, when heard, we'll discover a fulfilling sense of being alive. That's the 'will' of God for us.

Jesus and God's Will

Just as Mary sought to live out God's Will, so must all
Christians:

> 'Here am I, the servant of the Lord; let it be with me
> according to your word.'
> (Luke 1.38)

In Jesus who prayed 'thy will be done, on earth as it is in
heaven' (Matt. 6.10) we find one who came not to do his own
will but the Will of the Father (John 5.30), a Will he sought to
live even when facing his Passion as he prayed:

> 'Not my will but yours be done.'
> (Luke 22.42)

That's not being fatalistic but letting go of our egocentricity
and saying 'yes' to God. To daily live out the Divine Will
is to seek to live as Jesus taught. To find in him the person
whose life speaks of what it can mean to be fully human. To
commit our life to God and say 'yes' to co-operating with
God's creativeness. To allow ourselves to be used by God as
clay in the hands of a potter. To want to creatively 'flow' with
Divine desire – these are ways of prayerful living.

Some fear what might happen if they gave themselves –
abandoned themselves – to God and stopped worrying about
themselves (Matt. 6.31–34). Yet the One who loves us so
passionately wants nothing apart from our good. Praying
'thy will be done' means trusting that, in handing something
to God, God wants the very *best* that can happen. To desire
to live in the Will of God is simply to desire to live that life
opened for us in baptism.

Bend my heart to your will, O God –
By your word, give me life!
(cf. Psalm 119.36f.)

Saying 'yes' to journeying with Christ means turning to him
to see how to live. He's the one who reminds me that, loved
by God, I am to *be* love. He's the one who inspires me; who
kindly invites me to grow beyond the narrow constraints of
my-self; who shows me what this matter of 'human-being' is
meant to be like. And this will affect every aspect of my life.

Following Jesus does not mean slavishly copying his life.
It means making his choice of life your own,
starting from your own potential
and in the place where you find yourself.
It means living for the values
for which Jesus lived and died.
It means following the path he took
and seeing things as he saw them.[3]

Faith and politics

The New Testament is full of advice about how we should
live this 'life in Christ' and the Letter of James contains some
of the most radical instructions of all:

If a brother or sister is naked and lacks daily food, and
one of you says to them, 'Go in peace; keep warm and eat
your fill', and yet you do not supply their bodily needs,
what is the good of that? So faith by itself, if it has no
works, is dead.
(James 2.15–17)

That reflects Jesus' prophetic calling to 'bring good news to
the poor … to proclaim release to the captives and recovery

of sight to the blind, to let the oppressed go free' (Luke 4.18).
Our faith concerns God's demand that we care for people –
the 'polis' (Greek) – and speak out on behalf of the poor.

*When people say that the Bible and politics don't mix, I
ask them which Bible they are reading.*[4]

Every time we pray the Our Father and say 'thy kingdom
come' we're engaging in a political act, which isn't the same
as being involved in *party* politics but in the public affairs of a
society. Faith must embrace the *whole* of life; after Mary had
pondered the angel's message, she made her own the great
song of Hannah (1 Sam. 2.1–10), rejoicing in what God had
done in her and affirming that:

'He has brought down the powerful from their thrones,
and lifted up the lowly;
he has filled the hungry with good things,
and sent the rich away empty.'
(Luke 1.52–53)

Mary's response came from a contemplative heart and the
Church needs to nurture contemplative living because it roots
action in love. Action *without* contemplation risks giving
permission to the emergence of dark forces and a church
without contemplatives is in danger of becoming lost in activity. Pray for vocations to our contemplative communities.

Jesu, thou art all compassion

Living in a world where those forces are all-too-prevalent,
we need to heed a (slightly paraphrased) saying of the
nineteenth-century Russian monk, St Seraphim of Sarov:
'Have compassion in your heart and thousands around you
will be saved.' Faced with life-diminishing forces we're to

exemplify Divine compassion, to live out of Jesus' Heart: 'Those who say, "I love God", and hate their brothers or sisters, are liars; for those who do not love a brother or sister whom they have seen, cannot love God whom they have not seen' (1 John 4.20). Living with compassion isn't easy, it's not the same as kindness or simply being sympathetic: it involves desiring to be open to the world and meeting it with love in action.

One of my favourite Gospel stories is of the rich young man who came to Jesus with such enthusiasm because he 'wanted to inherit eternal life' but:

> *Jesus, looking at him, loved him and said, 'You lack one thing; go, sell what you own, and give the money to the poor, and you will have treasure in heaven; then come, follow me.' When he heard this, he was shocked and went away grieving, for he had many possessions.*
> *(Mark 10.21–22)*

What might he say if you were to ask him that question? We may have a deep desire to live the way of Christ yet often fail, but in a wonderful phrase of Julian of Norwich, Jesus looks on us 'with pity, not with blame'.[5] And when we can allow ourselves to sit in that gaze then, as St John of the Cross says in his Spiritual Canticle (32): 'his eyes imprint their grace in our soul'.

But, more wonderful still, what we see in Jesus is a reflection of what lies within us. We are to mirror aspects of that diamond-studded Divine Compassion that dwells in him; our being contains a reflection of the wonder he enfleshes.

Abiding in the Heart of Jesus

Christianity is pervaded by this 'aroma' of Jesus' love that needs to permeate *our* lives. We're those who seek to abide in his loving Heart as he abides in ours, and in that abiding – that remaining together – to form an intimate, loving relationship.

We've noted how St Paul tells us that Jesus is the 'image of the invisible God' and, for many, that image is to be found in the Sacred Heart of Jesus. There's something about the image of the heart which communicates powerfully, and for centuries the Church has recognized in the Sacred Heart an image revealing God's passionate love for all creation. What do you see in this Heart?

> O Sacred Heart of Jesus, fountain of eternal life,
> Your Heart is a glowing furnace of Love.
> You are my refuge and my sanctuary.[6]

The early Carmelites understood they were called to live out of the Heart of Jesus and realized the importance of developing a 'right' heart. They followed others who saw the heart as the 'cell' where we are to live and pray:

> Come, Lord, stir us up and call us back.
> Kindle and seize us.
> Be our fire and our sweetness. Let us love. Let us run.[7]

John Wesley, the founder of Methodism, on hearing Martin Luther's description of the change God works in the heart through faith in Christ found his own being 'strangely warmed'. Of that 'warming' he later said that it concerned: 'loving God with all our heart, and our neighbours as ourselves, and in that love abstaining from all evil, and doing all possible good to all men'.[8] And although the Church of England hasn't officially adopted this wonderful and important devotion it seeps through at times:

O dearest Lord, thy sacred heart
with spear was pierced for me;
O pour thy Spirit in my heart
that I may live for thee.[9]

Jesus clearly realized we need to plumb the depths of our heart wherein are streams of life – of love. Like many I find the story of Jesus' encounter with a woman at a well (John 4.5ff.) to be a powerful invitation to give attention to the heart, for the Heart of Jesus is an ocean of love.

Most Sacred Heart of Jesus,
have mercy upon us.

Following Christ

Christ's Heart draws us into a journey of love for all that God has made, yet Christianity isn't just about loving our neighbour – it's discovering that our true identity can only be realized through an ever-deepening relationship to God in Christ. Setting out can be exciting but as time goes on our initial enthusiasm will wane. It's then we need to seek God for God's sake and not for what we might get out of that relationship; this is the opportunity to grow in faith, hope and love, to allow ourselves to be filled with grace – the 'energies' of God.

St Teresa of Avila compared this to a journey into an 'Interior Castle' which is beset by many difficulties, yet the desire to encounter God who dwells at its heart means we can never give up. It's a life with the kingdom of God as its objective ('thy kingdom come') through cleansing of the heart ('thy will be done'); a kingdom of justice, peace and joy (Rom. 14.17) which is within us (Luke 17.21) through the Holy Spirit who calls us into ever deeper union with God.

For this reason, church 'growth' mustn't simply be about numbers. We may recognize the need to be 'reaching out' but are we 'reaching in'? Is the growth of violence in society partially due to having ignored our spiritual life, to the Church forgetting this primary calling? As we gradually awaken to the effects of excessive consumption, we need to give greater attention to the riches of the Christian spiritual tradition.

One of the most important things about Christianity is that it challenges us to ask questions about the way we live. St Paul told Christians in Rome that the essence of their life was to:

> *Let love be genuine; hate what is evil, hold fast to what is good; love one another with mutual affection; outdo one another in showing honour ... Rejoice in hope, be patient in suffering, persevere in prayer. Contribute to the needs of the saints; extend hospitality to strangers. Bless those who persecute you; bless and do not curse them. Rejoice with those who rejoice, weep with those who weep. Live in harmony with one another; do not be haughty, but associate with the lowly; do not claim to be wiser than you are. Do not repay anyone evil for evil, but take thought for what is noble in the sight of all. If it is possible, so far as it depends on you, live peaceably with all. Beloved, never avenge yourselves ... No, 'if your enemies are hungry, feed them; if they are thirsty, give them something to drink ...' Do not be overcome by evil, but overcome evil with good.*
> *(Romans 12.9–21)*

If God, full of love and compassion, is deeply concerned with the well-being of creation then we need to be filled with that same compassion for others. As the *Principles* of the Spiritual Association of the Compassionate Hearts of Jesus and Mary say: 'like all Christians (we) are called to a constant conversion of (our) hearts until they reflect the glory of God in whose image and likeness (we) are made. (We) must seek first the kingdom of God and his righteousness (Matt. 6.33) for where our treasure lies, there will our hearts be also (Matt. 6.21).'

Rule of Life

All this reminds me of the two 'laws' Jesus taught us to live by. To love:

- 'the Lord your God with all your heart, and with all your soul, and with all your mind.' This is the greatest and first commandment. And a second is like it:
- '(to love) your neighbour as yourself.' (Matt. 22.37f.)

and to:

- remember him through the Eucharistic feast ('do this in remembrance of me').

Consequently, Christians are encouraged to develop a 'rule of life'. Lots of people say they don't want 'rules and regulations' – isn't being a Christian all about being free? But the word 'rule', coming from the Latin *regula*, means regularizing life, staying on a chosen pathway. Rather than being constricting, it concerns some simple norms that lead to life in all its fullness (John 10.10).

You'll find some questions at the end of this chapter to help you draw up a personal Rule of Life, something you might talk through with a spiritual director.

Finally ...

So, what's it all about? Is life about being successful, gaining wealth, approval ... power? Christianity says that all those are false gods. What will, in the end, satisfy our heart is giving glory to our Creator through the way we live; realizing a deep sense of gratitude – of thanksgiving and praise – for life and nurturing a sense of compassion for all things, because we're learning to look at the world with the eye of the heart. Life's about turning from bitterness and despair to embrace faith, hope and love.

Christianity is a pathway to freedom, freedom from what St Paul calls 'the elemental forces of the universe' (Gal. 4.3, 8–9) which drive us towards sin and death. A path to that freedom of life in Christ who pours grace, the spiritual energies of the age to come, upon us and which Paul writes about with such passion (Rom. 8.21–39). Christ invites us to live in union with him: this is what God created humankind to enjoy – not anarchic freedom but the freedom that comes from living out of the Gospel, the freedom of the heirs of God. We are to be a new creation inseparable from Christ who is our life (2 Cor. 5.17) and, in that union, to find our joy.

> *Beloved, we are God's children now; what we will be has not yet been revealed. What we do know is this: when he is revealed, we will be like him, for we will see him as he is.*
> (*1 John 3.2*)

So be strong in the Lord, as Paul urges his readers, and let yourself be enfolded in him. And, as we venerate him in his Most Holy Sacrament and feed on his life, remember to reverence him through your love and care for the whole of creation. Contemplative love for the 'other' draws us more deeply into the *Heart* of the Other – of God – which Julian of Norwich realized when, on pondering the meaning of life, she discovered that 'love was His meaning'.[10] Remember the words of St John:

> *To all who received him, who believed in his name,*
> *he gave power to become children of God,*
> *who were born, not of blood or of the will of the flesh*
> *or of the will of man, but of God.*
> *And the Word became flesh and lived among us,*
> *and we have seen his glory,*
> *the glory as of a father's only son,*
> *full of grace and truth.*
> *(John 1.12–14)*

May you be filled with grace as you seek to follow Christ.

AMDG
(To the greater glory of God)

> *Take, Lord, and receive all my liberty,*
> *my memory, my understanding,*
> *and my entire will,*
> *All I have and call my own.*
> *You have given all to me.*
> *To you, Lord, I return it.*
> *Everything is yours; do with it what you will.*
> *Give me only your love and your grace,*
> *that is enough for me.*[11]

❧

Invitation:

Developing a Rule of Life. Here are some of the questions you might reflect on:

- What gives life to my relationship with God?
- What are the principles by which I seek to live?
- What prayer practices do I need to foster? (Daily Office/ Silent prayer/annual Retreat/Bible reading/spiritual reading ...)? How much time can I set aside, morning and evening? What are the best times I can identify?
- Apart from Sundays are there other times when I will try to attend the Eucharist and what would help me make sure that I am living with thanksgiving (eucharistically)?
- What relationships are important in my life and how do I need to nurture them?
- What guidelines can I identify that would help me grow in love for my spouse/partner, family, friends, colleagues and others? When will I make my Confession?
- How does the Reign of God (peace and justice, bringing healing, reconciliation and hope to my community, my church and the world) find expression in my life?
- How can I best employ my gifts in the service of God and for the benefit of others?
- What proportion of my income do I need to set aside for the benefit of others?
- How will I express my creativity and develop my mind (through reading, the arts, etc.)?
- How do I care for and nurture myself (e.g. by eating healthily, getting regular exercise and adequate sleep)?
- How can I incorporate times for rest, retreat and recreation into my day, week and year?

You'll probably need to spend a bit of time considering these before committing them to paper. And you'll need to revisit any Rule from time to time as your circumstances change. And remember, a Rule is for *life*; it's not meant to be a strait-jacket!

Notes

1 'The Pastoral Constitution on the Church in the Modern World' – *Gaudium et Spes*, 9, 1965.
2 The Spiritual Association of the Compassionate Hearts of Jesus and Mary.
3 *Rule for a New Brother*, 2, The Benedictine Nuns of Turvey Abbey, 1973.
4 Bishop Desmond Tutu (attributed, but unsourced). Cf. 'I don't preach a social gospel; I preach the Gospel, period. The gospel of our Lord Jesus Christ is concerned for the whole person. When people were hungry Jesus didn't say "Now is that political or social?" He said, "I feed you." Because the good news to a hungry person is bread.' As quoted in *God's Mission in the World: An Ecumenical Christian Study Guide on Global Poverty and the Millennium Development Goals* (2006) by The Episcopal Church Office of Government Relations and the Evangelical Lutheran Church in America.
5 *Revelations of Divine Love*, Chapter 28.
6 From a prayer to the Sacred Heart of Jesus by St Gertrude the Great (1256–1302).
7 St Augustine, *Confessions*, 8.4.
8 John Wesley, *The Works of the Reverend John Wesley, A. M.*, ed. J. Emory and B. Waugh, New York, 1831.
9 Fr Andrew SDC (1869–1946).
10 *Revelations of Divine Love*, ch. 86.
11 St Ignatius Loyola, from the *Spiritual Exercises*, 234.

Chapters 15 and 16

For reflection and discussion

- Jesus said: 'What does it profit them if they gain the whole world, but lose or forfeit themselves?' (Luke 9.25). What do these words say to you?
- When Jesus tells us to pray: 'thy kingdom come on earth, as it is in heaven', what do you think he meant?
- Stop. Look. Listen. What do you notice about the world around you? For what do you need to give thanks? And, when you do give thanks, how does that make you feel?
- What do you need to 'let go' of to God? What might help you do that?
- What instructions might you need to write concerning your funeral?

For we do not proclaim ourselves;
we proclaim Jesus Christ as Lord
and ourselves as your slaves for Jesus' sake.
For it is the God who said,
'Let light shine out of darkness',
who has shone in our hearts
to give the light of the knowledge of the glory of God
in the face of Jesus Christ.
2 Corinthians 4.5–6

Appendix 1

What is Spiritual Direction?

Spiritual Direction (sometimes called 'Spiritual Accompaniment' or 'Soul Friendship') is a confidential ministry whereby a person is helped to explore a deeper understanding of their relationship with God, the Divine Other, in the context of the world they inhabit.

It addresses the whole person but differs from counselling in being the process of accompanying someone on their journey into wholeness and holiness as they seek to respond to the deepening call of God. Like many therapeutic practices, it offers a safe, welcoming and confidential space in which life stories can be explored; it's non-judgemental and isn't about telling people how to behave but how to listen and respond to the movements going on within them.

It's an ongoing relationship needing time to understand the movements occurring in the life of an individual (the 'directee'). A useful image from Scripture might be the Journey to Emmaus (Luke 24.13–35) when two disciples travelled together until the Lord revealed himself to them.

What happens?

A typical session lasts up to an hour. The directee should consider how they want to use the time. One question they reflect on is: 'What movements in my inner life have I noticed occurring since we last met? How have I been conscious – or not – of God's activity in my life?' The session would then continue with your director inviting you to consider open, reflective questions, working with you to deepen your experience of the movement of God, helping you come to that place of freedom whereby you can make your response to the One who is calling you to ever deeper union. At times there may be some insights offered as the director will also be noticing the way the Spirit is working in themselves and in the directee. For, in the end, it is God who is the primary Director and both director and directee need to realize that they sit in that Divine, compassionate gaze.

More information can be found on the website of most dioceses or via the London Centre for Spiritual Direction (www.lcsd.org.uk).

Appendix 2

Some Ways of Developing Our Prayer

Prayer is our response to the Other
so that we are taken beyond ourselves
and grow into our full potential,
which is holiness.

Introduction

1 Find the right place to pray that fits what you need, e.g. quiet, still, etc. ... whatever leads you to be attentive and relaxed at the same time. Adopt a posture that helps you be attentive but relaxed. Some can lie down without sleeping; use a lotus/half lotus; sit on a prayer-stool. Many use an upright chair, sitting with your back against the upright support with both feet on the ground and hands resting in the lap.

2 All methods of prayer are means to an end, none work miracles. All methods need practice before you become at home in them. So, be patient ... don't be a butterfly!

3 Give time to the preliminaries of prayer. Settle into posture, still your body and mind. Recognize you are in the presence of the Divine; offer the time to God; ask for light and openness. Make the Sign of the Cross: 'Come, Holy Spirit ...'

Stillness or Awareness Prayer

Here are three methods among many. They can be just relaxing exercises; attentive preparations for other kinds of prayer; or, in themselves, a still, attentive, wordless prayer of presence.

Awareness of the Body

Starting from the crown of the head ... pass through the body to the feet. Feel the various parts of your body in turn ... the touch of clothes or chair, feet on the floor, etc. ... Allow time (a few seconds) for feelings in each part to become apparent. Identify, be aware, and pass on. Try to concentrate your whole attention in turn on each feeling. So ... head, face, neck, ears, etc. ... down to ankles, feet, sole, toes, each toe ... Do this two or three times.

More explicitly 'religious': recognize God's presence in your feelings ... in your body ... in you as a person.

Awareness of Sounds

Identify each sound you can hear. Don't rush, as many sounds only become apparent with attentive listening. Simply, without strain, concentrate your attention wholly on each sound in turn and move on. Sudden sounds, distractions, etc., should be acknowledged, not fought against. Then, with effort, bring your whole attention back to where you were before. For a sequence move from outside to inside the room. Finally, yourself ... your breathing ...

Don't rush and don't strain.

More explicitly 'religious': recognize God's presence in the sounds and what they symbolize ... people, nature, the wind as God's breath.

Breathing

Listen to your breathing. Don't alter the pace or depth just be aware ... I am breathing in ... I am breathing out ... Follow your breath into your body and try to concentrate all attention on this one action. If you get distracted don't fight it, acknowledge it and gently pass back to your breathing.

Possible religious dimensions: God is my breathing ... God is as the air ... all around ... within me ... I am breathing in God's life ... I am breathing in God's love ... and breathing out negativity and selfishness. Set up a gentle rhythm of breathing.

Or, link with a significant word/phrase. Ignatius Loyola suggests the 'Our Father' word by word, or phrase by phrase linked to each breath. Others suggest 'Ma-ra-na-tha', 'Come, Lord Jesus ...', 'Jesus ...', 'Lord Jesus Christ, Son of God, have mercy on me ...'

Praying with the Scriptures

Before either of these, still yourself, perhaps using one of the exercises above. Prepare your chosen passage by carefully reading it. Note any interesting intellectual questions, but leave that until after the prayer period.

Benedictine 'Lectio Divina', a savouring prayer

Slowly read a passage of Scripture until a word or phrase particularly strikes you. Then reread the passage and savour the word/words by vocally or mentally repeating it. Then be still and begin to speak to the Lord in whose presence you are; or, keep an attentive silence in his presence. Finally, simply rest in the Lord. (N.B. You don't have to finish the passage – you might not get beyond the first word.)

Ignatian 'Gospel Contemplation' or 'Imaginative Prayer'

The use of the imagination has a long history from the early Franciscans through to Ignatius Loyola. It's used to get in touch, now, with Gospel scenes. As a method it seeks to place you in the scene; no longer the observer but encountering Christ now ... the Word of God behind the words of Scripture.

- Take a Gospel scene. Read it carefully and familiarize yourself with it.
- Place yourself in the scene. Take time: use your senses (e.g. the Sea of Galilee: see it, smell the air, the fish ... get into a boat ... what's it like? Feel the motion, hear the sounds, words and so on). When the scene is fully present to you and you are feeling at home ...
- Let yourself be present in the story. You may become a central character, for example, Peter in the boat, someone asking for healing or a bystander. Some even change roles while meditating; often the unplanned is an indication that you are deeply involved. Hear the words spoken; see the people's actions and allow yourself to react. Don't worry if your imagination doesn't follow Scripture exactly and you find yourself as Peter unable to get out of the boat, for example. Address any questions you may have to Jesus.
- You may find that you talk with Christ and/or others quite naturally. In any case, when the 'scene' is over, take time to address Jesus or other characters in the story. Ask them their reactions and if there's something you don't understand, question them.

N.B. You're not seeking to be an observer, but to be IN the scene. Don't worry if you have problems and difficulties to start with, for example, if the scene is not clear; practice will help. Don't worry about historical detail or accuracy. This is *imaginative* and only a means to an end, an encounter with Christ.

Appendix 3

Suggestions for Using this Book

Apart from an 'Invitation' for personal use at the end of each chapter, this book is designed to accompany a Confirmation, Lent or general Study Course. For this reason, there are a series of 'Reflections' at regular intervals – after a series of chapters that need to be read and then discussed. In addition to those questions it can help to encourage people to broaden their reflection in different ways.

- As part of a reflection on creation, invite people to undertake a 'Walk of Thanksgiving and Praise'. A walk of about half an hour is suggested. First, take a few minutes to relax and allow yourself to become aware of the presence of the Spirit with you and all creation, and commit this time to God. As you step outdoors, take a deep breath of fresh air.
- When you have walked far enough to be out of earshot of anyone, pause to consciously experience the use of your:

Sight

Use your vision to really notice everything around you. Try to realize how different your life, and you, would be had you been born without this sense gift, or had you lost it.

Move on and then:

Hearing

Stop and listen, even to the seeming silence in all reality teeming with sounds, the sound of human voices, traffic, birdsong, etc. Listen for the sounds beneath the sounds.

Touch

Moving on, consciously experience the feel of the sun and air on your skin, the texture of clothing, grass, trees, stones, the awareness of the pull of gravity through the pressure of the ground under your feet; the sense of balance through this; reflect upon the use of touch in expressing affection, in physical work, in playing musical instruments, writing, etc.

Taste and smell

Repeat the exercises as above.

Return and, after reflecting on what you've encountered, write notes in a Journal or share with the group. How does this relate to God-in-all-things?

- As part of a reflection on the Passion, Resurrection, etc., invite people to visit an art gallery where there's a collection of religious paintings on these themes and spend time sitting with various works, noticing what they say to you. If you don't have access to a gallery, find appropriate pictures online and reflect on them before sharing with a group. Participants could also be invited to choose a piece of music which spoke to them of the Passion, for example, and introduce this to others.
- Draw a plan of your church. Invite people to name the different parts and what happens there. Discuss.

- Visit a monastery or convent and talk to a sister or brother about prayer. Join in the prayer life of the community. If you cannot do this, arrange to show a film such as *Into Great Silence*, a day in the life of the monks of La Grande Chartreuse, the Carthusian monastery high in the French Alps, and discuss what it says about prayer and life.
- Arrange a Week of Accompanied Prayer for people to join; this could be done together with other churches. Your diocesan Spirituality Adviser can help you with this.
- Show a film that reflects aspects of our Faith, for example *The Mission*, The Chronicles of Narnia – *The Lion, the Witch and the Wardrobe*, *The Shawshank Redemption*, *Harry Potter and the Deathly Hallows*, *The Lion King*. Invite people to reflect on their message.
- Find out about a local social project and invite people to reflect on how it might express aspects of Christian living.

&

I'm sure you can think of other creative ways in which themes dealt with in this book could be explored.

Appendix 4

GOOD FRIDAY
NIGHT LITURGY
OF THE DEPOSITION AND
BURIAL OF THE LORD

This liturgy, based on the ancient Office of Tenebrae and the Orthodox Festal Menaion (Service for Holy Saturday morning), celebrates the journey of Christ into the realm of Death and Hades and recognizes the effect of his redemptive work at both a conscious and unconscious level, for it affects the whole cosmic order. The place of the Mother of God and of Jesus' friends and allies is also celebrated, reminding us of the importance of these 'lesser' figures of the Passion.

A large crucifix stands on the altar. The church is in semi-darkness. A low table, representing the tomb of Christ and surrounded by candles and flowers, stands in the centre of the church. The liturgy begins with Night Prayer.

☙

THE PREPARATION

Off: The Lord almighty grant us a quiet night and a perfect end.

All: **Amen.**

Off: Blessed is the Kingdom of the Father +, and of the Son, and of the Holy Spirit.

All: **Amen. Glory to you, O Christ, glory to you!**

*A period of silence follows, for reflection on the past day,
after which a suitable form of confession is offered*

Off: + O God, make speed to save us.
All: **O Lord, make haste to help us.**

A suitable hymn is sung

THE WORD OF GOD

THE PSALMODY *Psalm 139.1–18 and Psalm 3*

(The Gloria is not said)

A READING

The whole of creation was changed when it saw you, O
Christ, hanging on the Cross. The sun was darkened, and
the foundations of the earth were shaken; all things suffered
with the Creator of all. Of your own will you have endured
this for our sakes: Glory to you, Lord, glory to you!

THE RESPONSE

Off: Save me, O God, for the waters are come up, even
         to my throat.
All: **They gave me poison for food; and when I was
         thirsty, they gave me vinegar to drink.**

COMMEMORATION OF THE SORROWFUL MOTHER

THE HOLY GOSPEL

Off 1: + A reading from the holy Gospel according to John (19.31–42)

A short period of reflective silence follows

Off 2: Gracious Lord, may your divine light shine upon those who lovingly seek you: may they know you, O Christ, as true God who calls them from the depths of hell.

Off 1: Broken and deeply grieving, Joseph of Arimathea and Nicodemus took down the body of their Master from the Cross. The Blessed Virgin Mother wept as he was laid on her knees; her tears flowed onto him and, in her grief, she bent down and kissed him:

All: **'My Son, my God, you were my only hope, my life and the light of my eyes; now I have lost you, my dearest and most beloved child!'**

Off 1: None can see God, on whom the angels dare not gaze; yet through you, the all-pure Virgin, the Word took human flesh and revealed himself to us.

All: **With all the hosts of heaven we magnify him, and we call you blessed.**

Off 2: 'Now heal my soul's wound, O my beloved Child. Rise and quieten my pain and grief. For you are all-powerful, O my Master, and can perform what you will.'

All: 'Have you not seen the depths of my love?' Christ said to his Virgin Mother. 'Because I wish to save all peoples, I have accepted to die. But I shall rise again and as God shall glorify you in heaven and on earth.'

Off 1: Going down to hell, O Life immortal, you have slaughtered hell with the light of your Divinity. And when you have raised up the departed from their dwelling place, all the powers of heaven cried aloud:

All: 'Praise the Lord, all you nations!'

COMMEMORATION OF THE DESCENT FROM THE CROSS

The Cross is taken from the altar and placed on the table. It is covered with the cloth and sprinkled with holy water. People gather around and all unnecessary lights are put out.

Off 2: Joseph of Arimathea, taking your body from the tree, wrapped it in clean linen with fragrant spices, and laid it in a new tomb.

All: **Blessed are they whose way is blameless, who walk in the law of the Lord.**

Off 2: When you, the Saviour of all, were laid for the sake of all in a new tomb, hell was derided and, seeing you, withdrew in fear. The bars of hell were broken and Adam in thanksgiving sang:

All: **'Bless the Lord, O my soul, and all that is within me bless his holy name.'**

Off 1: The Master of all lies in death, and in a new tomb he is placed, who empties the graves of the dead.

All: I will praise you with an upright heart, when I
        learn your righteous judgements.

Off 2: The flesh of God is now hidden beneath the earth,
        like a candle in a barrel, and it drives away the
        darkness in hell.

A candle is extinguished

All: I live as an alien in the land; do not hide your
        commandments from me.

Off 1: The whole creation was changed by your Passion:
        for all things suffered with you knowing, O
        Word, that you hold all things together in one.

All: My soul melts away for sorrow, O raise me up
        according to your word.

Off 2: You came down to earth, O Master, to save
        Adam: and not finding him there, you have
        sought him in hell.

A candle is extinguished

All: Guide me in the path of your commandments for
        therein is my delight.

Off 1: Uplifted on the Cross, you have uplifted all the
        living with yourself; and then, descending beneath
        the earth, raised those who were buried there.

Off 2: Willingly, O Saviour, you have descended beneath
        the earth and have restored the dead to life,
        leading them back in triumph to the glory of the
        Father.

A candle is extinguished

All: **Your word is a lamp to my feet and a light upon my path. Let me live that I may praise you, and let your judgements help me.**

Off 1:   O Word and God of all, in our hymns we praise you with the Father and your Holy Spirit, and we glorify your divine burial.

A candle is extinguished followed by silence. A loud noise is then made, symbolizing the earthquake that followed Christ's death.

Off 1:   May he who, for us and for our salvation, endured in the flesh the dread Passion, the life-giving Cross + and the burial among the dead, Christ our true God, grant us his blessing + now and for ever and to the ages of ages. **Amen.**

All depart in silence

Further Information

Information about lay Religious Associations: http://anglicans online.org/resources/orders.html

SLG Press produces excellent, reasonably priced pamphlets and booklets on a variety of aspects of Christian spirituality.

The Spiritual Association of the Compassionate Hearts of Jesus and Mary. An online, ecumenical association offering resources for the 'conversion of the heart'.

Further Reading

à Kempis, T., *The Imitation of Christ*, Penguin Classics, 2013.

de Caussade, J.-P., *Self-Abandonment to Divine Providence*, TAN Books, 1987.

de Sales, St Francis, *Introduction to the Devout Life*, Dover Publications Inc., 2009.

Dunstan, Peta, *Anglican Religious Life* (A yearbook of religious orders and communities, tertiaries, oblates, associates and companions), Canterbury Press, 2017.

Green, Thomas H., *Opening to God*, Ave Maria Press, 1987.

Hughes SJ, Gerald W., *God of Surprises*, DLT, 1985.

John of the Cross, St, *Sayings of Light and Love*, Westminster Roman Catholic Diocesan Trust, 2011.

Julian of Norwich, *Revelations of Divine Love*, tr. C. Wolters, Oxford University Press, 2015.

Laird, Martin, *Into the Silent Land – The Practice of Contemplation*, DLT, 2006.

Laurence, Brother *The Practice of the Presence of God*, Dover Publications, 2005.

Lewis, C. S., *Mere Christianity*, HarperCollins, 2015.

Lewis, C. S., *The Screwtape Letters*, HarperCollins, 2012.

Linn, D., S. and M., *Sleeping with Bread*, Paulist Press, 1995 *(Ignatian examen)*.

Martin SJ, M., *The Jesuit Guide to (Almost) Everything*, Harper One, 2010.

Stebbing CR, Nicolas, *Anglican Religious Life*, Dominican Publications, 2007.

Vanstone, W. H., *The Stature of Waiting*, DLT, 1982.

Vanstone, W. H., *Love's Endeavour, Love's Expense*, DLT, 2007.

Weil, S., *Waiting for God*, Fount, 1983.

Williams, R., *Being Christian*, SPCK, 2015.

The Cloud of Unknowing (author unknown, fourteenth century), Penguin Classics, 2001.

Acknowledgement of Sources

Scripture quotations are from the New Revised Standard Version of the Bible Anglicized edition © 1989 by the Division of Christian Education of the National Council of the Churches of Christ in the USA. Used by permission. All rights reserved.

The Revised Grail Psalms, copyright © 2010, Conception Abbey/The Grail, admin. by GIA Publications, Inc. www.giamusic.com. All rights reserved.

I am extremely grateful to the following for permission to quote from their works:

The Sisters of the Love of God for permission to quote extracts from *A Pilgrim's Book of Prayers* by Fr Gilbert Shaw, SLG Press, 2007.

The Ministers General of the Society and Community of St Francis for permission to quote from *Jacopone* by Br Ramon SSF and a verse from *The Blessing of Light* in The Daily Office SSF.

Libreria Editrice Vaticana for permission to quote from the *Catechism of the Catholic Church* (607), *Gaudete et Exsultate* (37) and from *Laudato Si* (217).

Anne Frank Fonds, Basel, Switzerland for permission to quote from *The Diary of Anne Frank*.

The Olivetan Benedictine nuns at Turvey Abbey for permission to quote from *Rule for a New Brother*.

Penguin Classics for permission to quote from *Aurora Leigh* by Elizabeth B. Browning.

Permission to use illustrations under copyright is acknowledged with thanks.

p. xxv   by Frater5, https://commons.wikimedia.org/wiki/
File:Sacredheart.svg

p. 22   http://theclipartwizard.com/holy-trinity-coloring-pages.htm

p. 31   http://www.clipartbest.com/search?q=Holy+Family

p. 38   http://clipart-library.com/clipart/98312.htm

p. 45   http://clipart-library.com/clipart/pT7K4078c.htm

p. 62   https://www.clipart.email/download/206122.html

p. 66   http://clipart-library.com/pascha-cliparts.html

p. 68   Source unknown

p. 71   Sixth-century icon in Saint Catherine's Monastery,
Mount Sinai, https://commons.wikimedia.org/w/index.
php?curid=489650

p. 84   http://1.bp.blogspot.com/-7sWVJK-s9Fc/TdLQV1pBDfI/
AAAAAAAAB4/MhUVEd4zoH4/s1600/10Holy%2BSpirit.
jpg

p. 103   https://www.kisspng.com/png-monstrance-clip-art-eucharist-
blessed-sacrament-on-7033689/preview.html

p. 124   http://playmasters.info/coloring/a/all-saints-day-coloring-
pages-for-kids.html

p. 133   Workshop of Ráckeve, God's mother with chosen saints,
c. 1760, Greek Orthodox Church, Miskolc, photo by
Szilas, https://commons.wikimedia.org/wiki/File:God%27s_
mother_%22showing_the_way%22_with_chosen_saints.jpg

p. 142   https://pixy.org/830935/

p. 152   http://www.liturgytools.net/2016/03/pictures-easter-sunday-
year-a-b-c-resurrection-new-life.html

p. 167   http://clipart-library.com/jesus-heart-cliparts.html

p. 186   Source unknown